*Yanmar*

# YANMAR MARINE DIESEL ENGINE MODEL SKE

*Service Manual*

*Yanmar*

**YANMAR MARINE DIESEL ENGINE MODEL SKE**

*Service Manual*

ISBN/EAN: 9783954272983
Erscheinungsjahr: 2013
Erscheinungsort: Bremen, Deutschland

© maritimepress in Europäischer Hochschulverlag GmbH & Co. KG, Fahrenheitstr. 1, 28359 Bremen. Alle Rechte beim Verlag und bei den jeweiligen Lizenzgebern.

www.maritimepress.de | office@maritimepress.de

Bei diesem Titel handelt es sich um den Nachdruck eines historischen, lange vergriffenen Buches. Da elektronische Druckvorlagen für diese Titel nicht existieren, musste auf alte Vorlagen zurückgegriffen werden. Hieraus zwangsläufig resultierende Qualitätsverluste bitten wir zu entschuldigen.

# YANMAR
## SERVICE MANUAL

MODEL
**SKE**

# CONTENTS

I. General Description .................................................... 1

    1. Name of Parts ..................................................... 1
    2. Data and Settings ................................................. 2
    3. Piping Diagram .................................................... 3
    4. Dimensions ........................................................ 4

II. Installation ........................................................... 5

III. Power Transfer (Power Take Off) ....................................... 10

IV. General Servicing ..................................................... 12

    1. Main Points of Servicing .......................................... 12
    2. Time of Periodic Cecks ............................................ 15
        2-1 Table of periodic checks ..................................... 16
        2-2 Every 50 hours ............................................... 18
        2-3 Every 250 hours .............................................. 18
        2-4 Every 500 hours .............................................. 19
        2-5 Every 1500 hours ............................................. 28
        2-6 Other time interval check .................................... 31
    3. Electric Wiring ................................................... 34

V. Maintenance Standards for Main Components .............................. 36

    1. Engine Disassembly Precautions .................................... 36
    2. Clearance & Tolerance of Main Components .......................... 40
    3. Exchange Standards for Wear of Main Parts ......................... 42
    4. Specified Tightening Torque for Major Parts ....................... 45

VI. Trouble Shooting ...................................................... 46

VII. Fuel Feed Pump ....................................................... 55

VIII. List of Approved Oil ................................................. 57

# I. General Description

1. **Name of Parts**

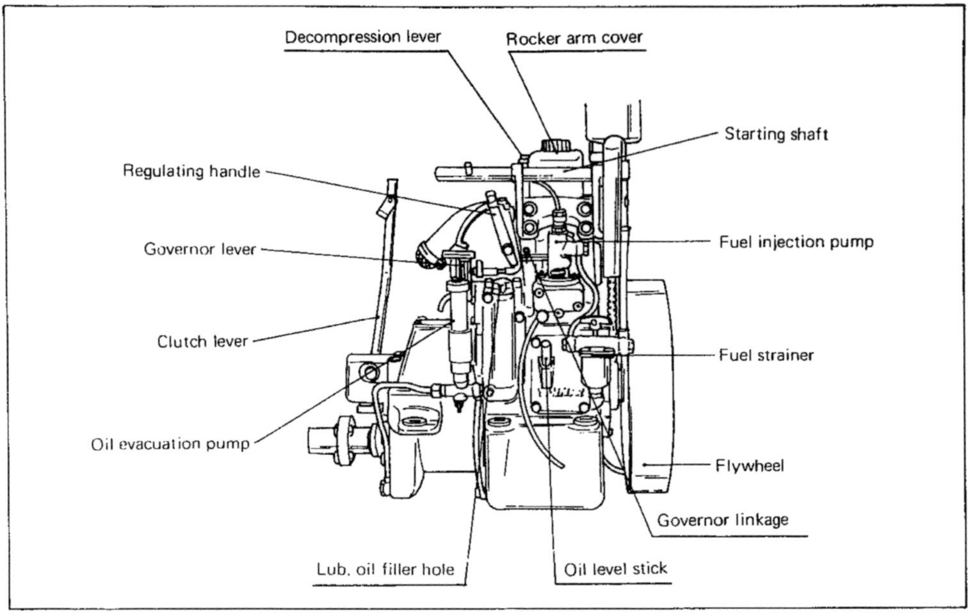

Decompression lever
Rocker arm cover
Regulating handle
Starting shaft
Governor lever
Fuel injection pump
Clutch lever
Fuel strainer
Oil evacuation pump
Flywheel
Governor linkage
Lub. oil filler hole
Oil level stick

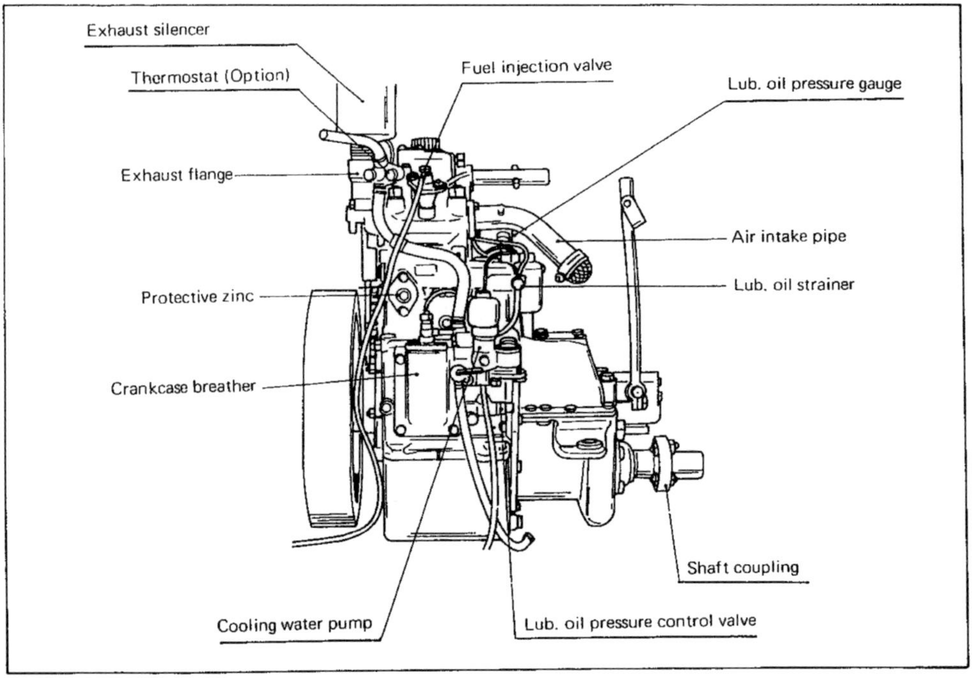

Exhaust silencer
Thermostat (Option)
Fuel injection valve
Lub. oil pressure gauge
Exhaust flange
Air intake pipe
Protective zinc
Lub. oil strainer
Crankcase breather
Shaft coupling
Cooling water pump
Lub. oil pressure control valve

## 2. Data and Settings

**ENGINE DATA**

| Model | SKE |
|---|---|
| Type | Vertical, single cyl. 4-cycle diesel |
| No. of Cylinders | 1 |
| Rated Engine Speed (rpm) | 2,400 |
| Cylinder bore x stroke (mm) | 92 x 100 |
| Direction of rotation — Crank shaft | Counter clockwise, viewed from stern |
| Direction of rotation — Propeller shaft | Clockwise, viewed from stern |
| Combustion system | Pre-combustion chamber type |
| Lubrication system | Forced lubrication by gear type pump |
| Cooling system | Forced circulation by plunger type pump |
| Starting system | Hand or Electric |
| Reduction/Reverse Gear | Mechanical/wet, single disc type |

**SETTINGS**

| Valve clearance | | Cold engine | 0.15 mm |
|---|---|---|---|
| Intake valve | Open | Before Top Dead Center (TDC) | 21° |
| Intake valve | Closed | Past Bottom Dead Center (BDC) | 45° |
| Exhaust valve | Open | Before Bottom Dead Center (BDC) | 48° |
| Exhaust valve | Closed | Past Top Dead Center (TDC) | 18° |
| *Fuel injection timing (start) | | Before Top Dead Center (BDC) | 12° ±1° |
| Fuel injection pressure (start) | | | 160 kg/cm$^2$ |
| Oil pressure (hand start) | | Engine speed at 2,400 rpm | 2-2.5 kg/cm$^2$ |

\* Confirm fuel injection timing by removing the high pressure fuel delivery pipe and positioning the fuel pump rack at the two dot mark.

## 3. Piping Diagram

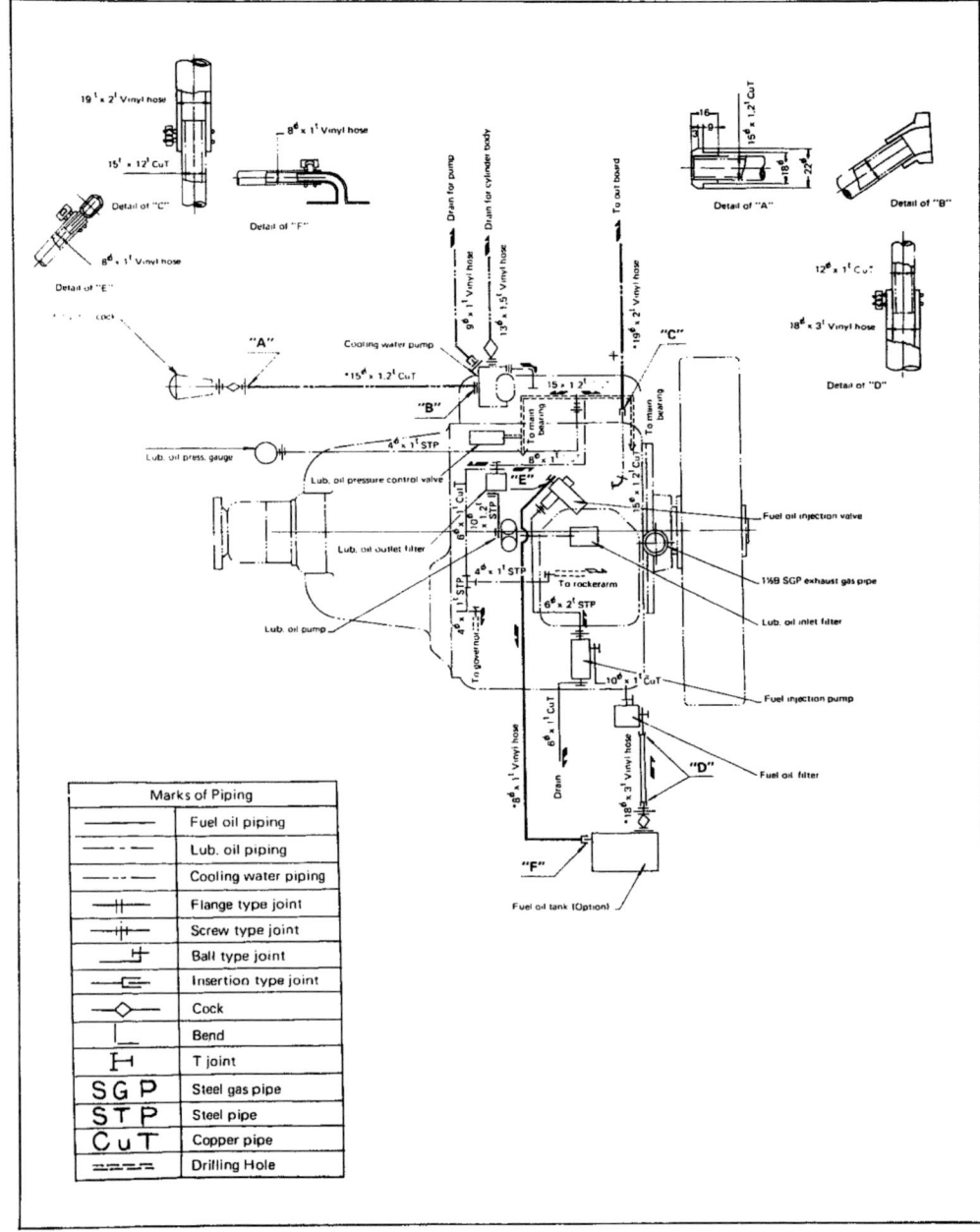

## 4. Dimensions

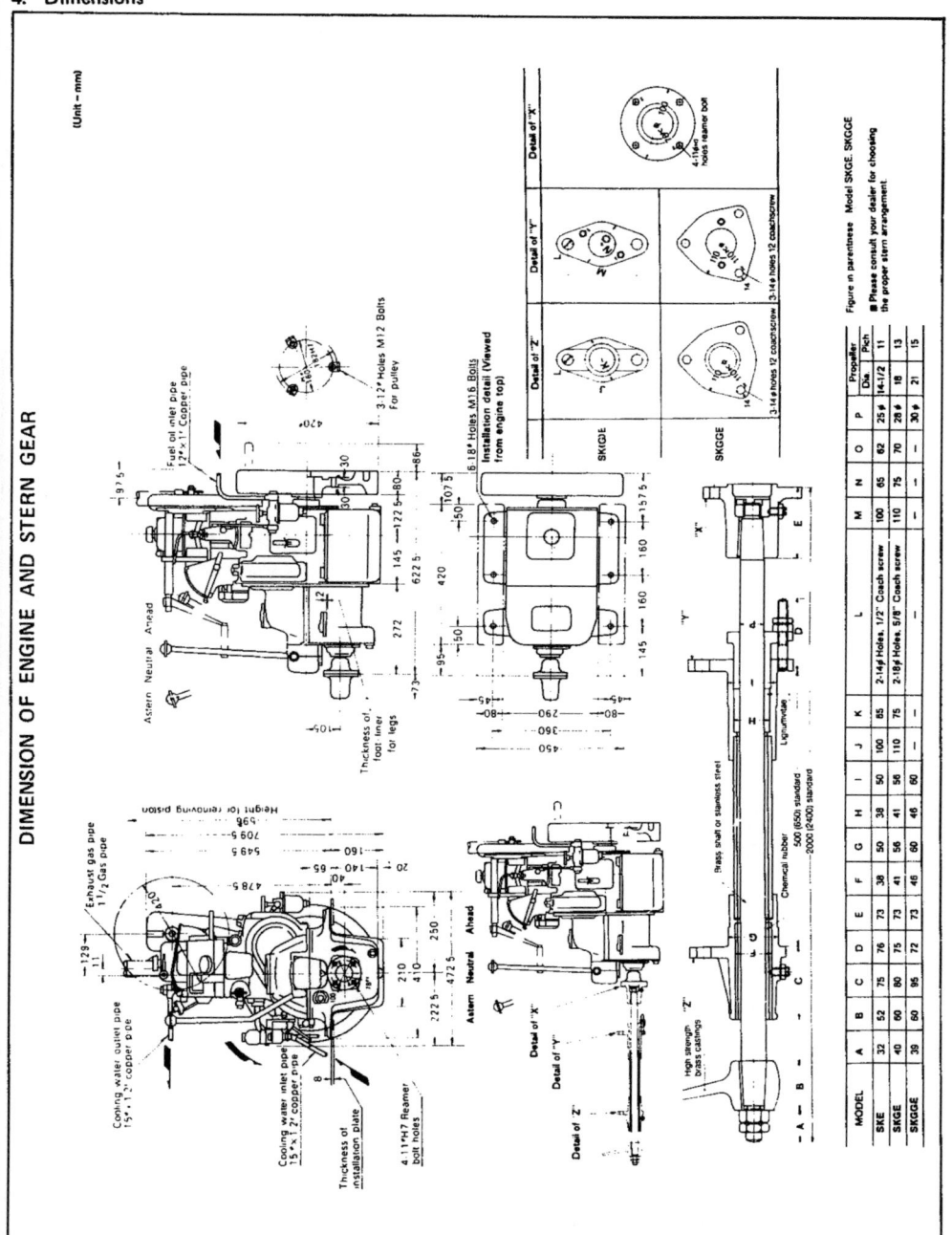

## II. Installation

**Engine Installation**

Installation of the engine is a most important factor in engine operation. Correct installation dictates superior performance and a long service life. Incorrect installation will result in poor operation, re-occurring maintenance problems, and a short service life.
Repeated problems with main bearings and the crank shaft are usually the result of improper engine installation. To avoid such problems, engine installation should be made with close attention given to installation instructions, and with sufficient time alloted.

General Installation Instructions

| Item | Procedure | Check Points |
|---|---|---|
| Rake | Less than 8°  Waterline  Propeller shaft | 1) Install the engine bed so that it forms a rake angle of less than 8° when water borne.<br><br>Note: Excessive rake angle results in loss of engine power due to improper prop angle. |
| Depth of propeller submersion | 0.8–1.0 D  Waterline  D | 1) Depth is roughly equivalent to the diameter of the propeller, with the ship not underway. (0.8D at least)<br><br>Note: A shallow propeller depth causes loss of speed due to increased slipping, as well as severe vibrations. |
| Wave hold-down board | (Example)  Parallel to propeller shaft  About 0.2 D   D | Effective in following cases:<br>1) Propeller too large to allow sufficient submersion.<br>2) More speed required.<br>3) Stern plunges too much when underway.<br><br>Note: Determine installation and dimensions according to size and use of the particular ship. |

| Item | Procedure | Check Points |
|---|---|---|
| Installation of stern tube | Tube housing block, Stern tube, Shaft axis, Lignumvitae or rubber | 1) Carefully check square crossing of the shaft axis and end surface of the tube housing which holds the stern tube.<br>2) When installing the stern tube in the tube housing, tentatively install the tube and align roughly with the engine, then tighten firmly.<br><br>Note: If the square crossing is inaccurate, or the stern tube is completely installed initially, engine alignment will be difficult later. |
| Selection of engine bed and installation | Engine bed, Frame | 1) Use hard materials.<br>2) Use pieces as large as possible.<br>3) Attach securely to hull and frame.<br>① Insure both ends are joined firmly to the frame and engine room bulkheads.<br>4) Insure shape is suitable for engine installation. |
| Installation of sea cock | Kingston cock, Inboard packing, Forward, Screen, Outboard packing | 1) Install so that the propeller does not suck air when the ship lists.<br>2) Install as close to the inlet of the cooling water pump as possible.<br>3) Position the Kingston cock so that inlet piping can be installed easily.<br>4) Position the suction inlet so that the open mouth slants down and aft.<br>5) Use canvas or rubber for inboard and outboard packings.<br>6) Be sure to apply liquid seal or paint to the canvas or rubber packings used.<br>7) Install a filter screen when the water contains floating objects or has a high silt content. |

| Item | Procedure | Check Points |
|---|---|---|
| Loading the engine | Exhaust pipe flange | Rig the engine as shown in the figure at left.<br>The bottom portion of the exhaust pipe flange serves as a hoist point. |
| Alignment | Differnce in clearances<br>Gap approx. 1 mm<br>Propeller shaft<br>Feeler gage<br><br>Check clearance variation between coupling surfaces around the periphery with a feeler gage.<br><br>Deviation — Steel scale<br>Gap approx. 5 mm<br><br>Confirm shaft height adjustment by checking for smooth engagement | 1) Tighten engine hold-down bolts lightly.<br>2) Variations in clearances between coupling surfaces should be less than 0.05 mm at each point.<br>3) Deviations in coupling peripherial surfaces should be less than 0.55 mm.<br>① Adjustments in athwartships deviations: move the engine athwartships as required.<br>② Vertical deviation adjustment: Align by adjusting thickness and/or number of shims under clutch mounting feet.<br><br>Note: Insert suitable number of shims if gap exists between engine mount feet and engine bed.<br><br>4) Adjustment when waterborne: Check engine alignment again when the ship is afloat. |

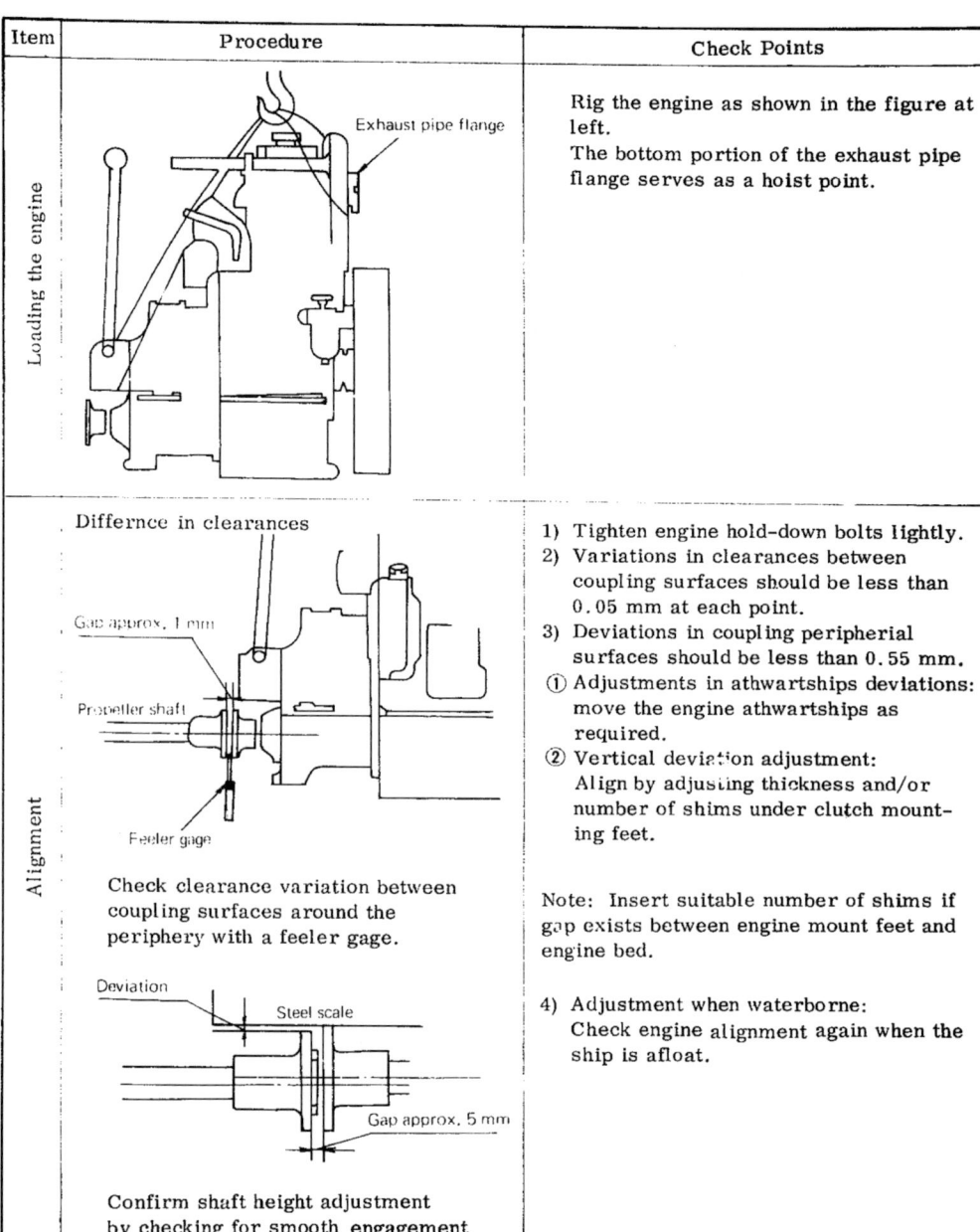

| Item | Procedure | Check Points |
|---|---|---|
| Cooling water piping installation | Support, Hose clamp, Cooling water pump, Cooling water inlet pipe, Kingston cock, Curvature over 30 R | 1) Always use copper tubing for the water inlet pipe.<br>2) Use vinyl hose for the intermediate section of the cooling water outlet piping and attach securely with hose clamps. Install hose supports to reduce vibrations.<br><br>Note: Vibrations will cause piping to crack and/or break.<br><br>3) Install both inlet and outlet piping as level as possible. Avoid vertical deviations.<br><br>Note: Insufficient cooling water may be supplied if a radical displacement in the piping system is made. |
| Installation of exhaust pipe and muffler | Flange, Insulator, Exhaust pipe, Hull | 1) Give close attention to vibration prevention and heat insulation during installation of exhaust pipe and muffler.<br><br>Note: The exhaust pipe and muffler may break at the point of connection, according to operating conditions.<br><br>① Installation of a flange as shown in the figure at left is recommended to prevent vibration.<br>② Keep the clearance between exhaust pipe and insulator as small as possible. (about 1-3 mm) |

| Item | Procedure | Check Points |
|---|---|---|
| Fuel tank installation | 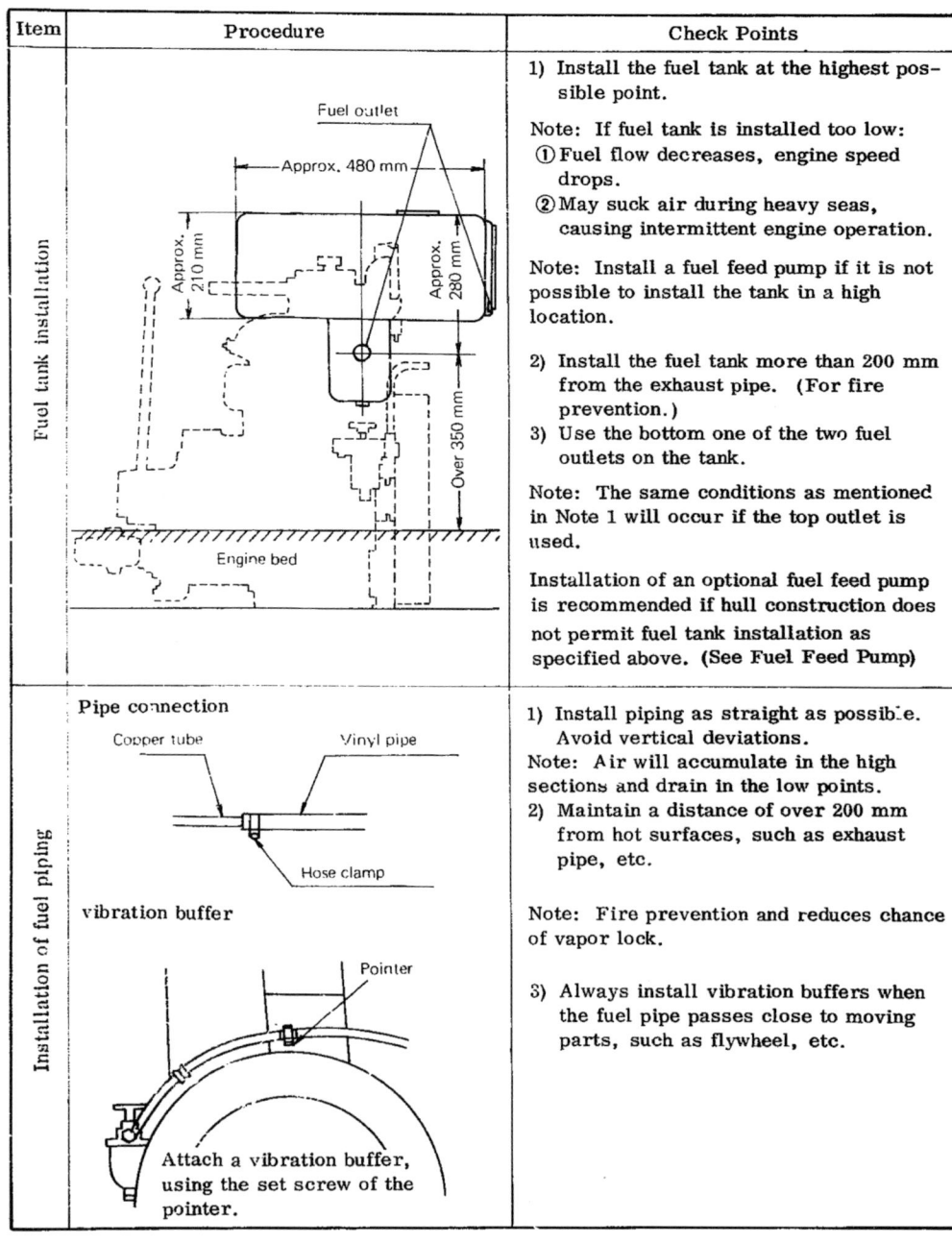 Fuel outlet — Approx. 480 mm — Approx. 210 mm — Approx. 280 mm — Over 350 mm — Engine bed | 1) Install the fuel tank at the highest possible point.<br><br>Note: If fuel tank is installed too low:<br>① Fuel flow decreases, engine speed drops.<br>② May suck air during heavy seas, causing intermittent engine operation.<br><br>Note: Install a fuel feed pump if it is not possible to install the tank in a high location.<br><br>2) Install the fuel tank more than 200 mm from the exhaust pipe. (For fire prevention.)<br>3) Use the bottom one of the two fuel outlets on the tank.<br><br>Note: The same conditions as mentioned in Note 1 will occur if the top outlet is used.<br><br>Installation of an optional fuel feed pump is recommended if hull construction does not permit fuel tank installation as specified above. (See Fuel Feed Pump) |
| Installation of fuel piping | Pipe connection<br>Copper tube   Vinyl pipe<br>Hose clamp<br><br>vibration buffer<br>Pointer<br><br>Attach a vibration buffer, using the set screw of the pointer. | 1) Install piping as straight as possible. Avoid vertical deviations.<br>Note: Air will accumulate in the high sections and drain in the low points.<br>2) Maintain a distance of over 200 mm from hot surfaces, such as exhaust pipe, etc.<br><br>Note: Fire prevention and reduces chance of vapor lock.<br><br>3) Always install vibration buffers when the fuel pipe passes close to moving parts, such as flywheel, etc. |

## III. Power Transfer (Power Take Off)

| Item | Procedure | Check Points |
|---|---|---|
| Power transfer | 1) Power transfer methods<br>A. Transfer power by attaching a pulley to the flywheel.<br><br>*[Diagram: Engine – Flywheel – Pulley]*<br><br>B. Install a pulley and a counter bearing.<br><br>*[Diagram: Engine – Pulley – Bearing]*<br><br>2) Amount of power transfer<br>Table of engine speed versus possible power transfer. | 1) Maximum power available from the forward end of an engine is limited by the method of transfer in large engines, but transfer of up to 11HP/2,400 rpm is possible in method A with this engine, if the propeller is not driven.<br><br>2) Relation between maximum horsepower and possible power transfer.<br><br>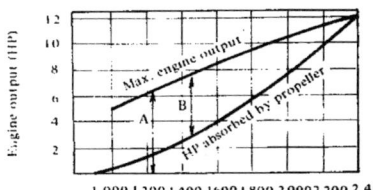<br><br>A: Power transferable when propeller is not driven.<br>B: Power transferable when propeller is driven.<br><br>3) Select specifications for engine load and diameter of pulley so that an engine speed of less than 800 rpm is not required.<br><br>4) Select an engine speed and load combination that is not too large.<br>Normal:  1 : 1~1 : 3<br>Maximum: 1 : 5 |

| Crankshaft revolutional speed | Engine output (maximum) | Propeller not driven | | Propeller driven | | |
|---|---|---|---|---|---|---|
| | | Possible power transfer | | Power required for propeller | Possible power transfer | |
| rpm | HP | HP | KW | HP | HP | KW |
| 1000 | 4.5 | 4.0 | 3   | 0.8  | 3.4 | 2.4 |
| 1200 | 5.5 | 5.0 | 3.7 | 1.5  | 3.6 | 2.6 |
| 1500 | 7.2 | 6.5 | 4.8 | 3.0  | 3.8 | 2.8 |
| 1800 | 8.8 | 8.0 | 6   | 5.2  | 3.3 | 2.4 |
| 2000 | 9.8 | 9.0 | 6.6 | 6.8  | 2.8 | 2   |
| 2400 | 12.0| 10.8| 8   | 12.0 | 0   | 0   |

Note: Level of power transfer values shown in the table are when engine load is by belts, as shown in Item 1 above.

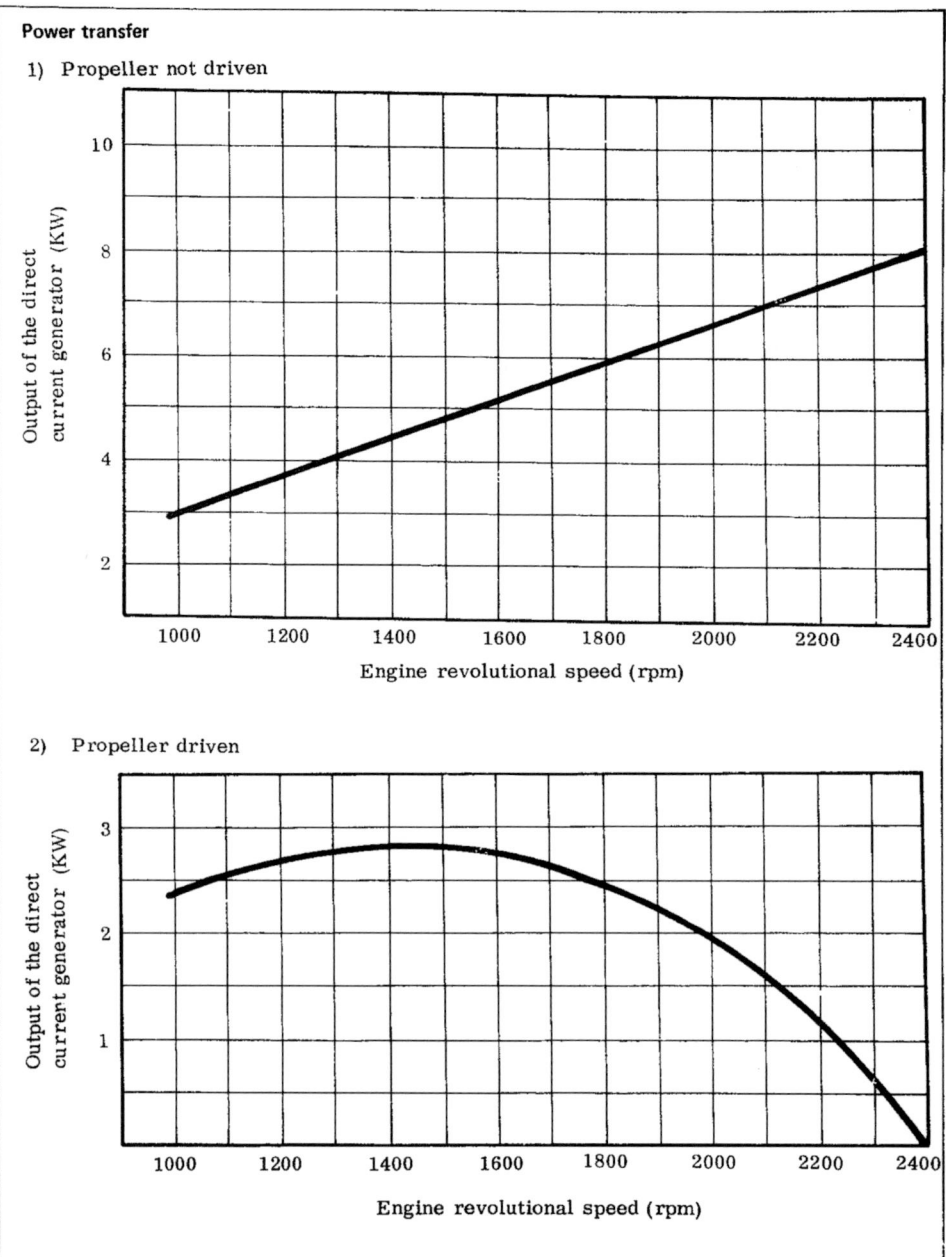

# IV. General Servicing

## 1. Main Points of Servicing

Daily servicing and periodical checking are necessary to maintain the engine in good condition. When delivering the engine, it is advisable to thoroughly explain to each user the handling and servicing procedures by using the service manual in which the main points of handling and periodic checks are given.

| | Treatment | Instruction to engine operator | Reason |
|---|---|---|---|
| | Selection and storage of fuel. | Use approved diesel fuel listed in list of approved oils. Avoid exposing the fuel to the sun. Keep sealed from dust. Strictly avoid using sedimentary fuel. | |
| | Selection and storage of engine oil. | Use approved engine lubricating oil listed in list of approved oils. Avoid exposing it to the sun. Keep sealed from dust. | Inferior quality oil may cause rapid wear and unnecessary damage. |
| Preparation prior to use | Check each nut and bolt. | Check for oil and water, and clogging. | |
| | Retighten, if necessary. | Retighten, if necessary. | |
| | Check and fill with engine oil, if required. | Fill until oil reaches the F-mark on oil level stick. | No, or low supply of oil causes seizure of moving parts. |
| | Check and fill with fuel, if required. | Avoid dust. Do not use sedimentary oil. | Foreign matter causes damage and wear to parts of fuel system. |
| | Oil each part. | 1. Fuel injection pump regulating rack. 2. Plunger parts of water pump and bilge pump. 3. Pinion shaft of cell motor. 4. Moving part of remote control device; shaft part of handle. | To help smooth movement of each part and to prevent seizure. |
| | Check openings of fuel and engine oil strainers. | Turn the handles a few times. | To clean clogged elements. |
| Operation | Hand operation before starting | Set the regulator handle at the "Stop" position, allowing no compression, and turn the flywheel by hand about ten times. | Permeate oil through each part to attain smooth operation. Confirm that no abnormal sounds are heard. |

| | Treatment | Instruction to engine operator | Reason |
|---|---|---|---|
| Operation | Turning | Set the reverse handle at "Neutral" and the regulator handle at "Stop", allowing no compression, and then push the starting switch to turn the cell motor through about ten revolutions. | |
| | Priming (confirmation of fuel injection) | Set the regulator handle at the "Run" position and move it from side by priming handle four or five times. The injection sound "betzu, betzu, ..." can be heard. When no such sound is heard, ventilate the fuel injection device. | |
| | Use of gasoline in cold weather | When starting is extremely difficult, supply gasoline to the suc. inlet cover. Do not supply too much. | |
| Caution in operation | Confirmation of oil pressure | Ahead, by 2,400 rpm; 1. Eng. oil pressure is $2 \sim 2.5$ $kg/cm^2$. | |
| | Warming-up | Run under no-load conditions at 600 $\sim$ 800 rpm for more than five minutes to warm up the engine. | To attain thorough oil permeation. To prevent the liner and piston from seizing due to a sudden increase in temperature immediately after starting. |
| | Confirmation of cooling water | Confirm whether the circulation of cooling water is normal or not. | Prevention of seizure. |
| | Confirmation of lube oil | Remove the bonnet, and confirm whether the circulation of eng. oil is normal or not around the valve lever shaft and valve arm guide. | Prevention of seizure. |
| | Observe color of exhaust gas | 1. Colorless to blueish white; engine in the best condition. 2. Black; a problem in the engine or overloaded. 3. White; eng. oil is burning. 4. Continuous black exhaust smoke should be avoided. | |

| | Treatment | Instruction to engine operator | Reason |
|---|---|---|---|
| Caution in operation | Check for abnormal sounds or abnormal increases in temperature. | When abnormal sounds or abnormal increases in temperature are observed, stop operation immediately and check the causes. | If not checked immediately, unnecessary damage may occur. |
| | Check for gas and water leakage. | Check for gas and water leakage, retighten bolts and nuts if necessary. | |
| | Avoid resonance. | At a certain number of revolutions, resonance between the engine and the frame may occur depending upon the structure of the frame. | Avoid operating the engine at the power setting at which resonance occurs, otherwise the engine will be subjected to undesirable effects. |
| | Check charge lamp. | If charge lamp does not go off even after high speed operation is reached, charging circuit is malfunctioning. | |
| | Fill with fuel. | Fill with fuel while the fuel level can still be seen on the fuel tank level gauge. | In case the engine stops due to fuel exhaustion, ventilation of the fuel pump is necessary after refilling with fuel. |
| Engine stop | Idle operation before engine stoppage. | Run at idle for about five minutes by placing the clutch in the "Neutral" position. Run at high speed momentarily before stopping the engine. | Discharge carbon in the combustion chamber from the engine. |
| | Engine stoppage. | Use the regulator handle to stop the engine. | If decompression handle is used to stop the engine, unburned fuel will accumulate in the cylinder, causing carbon build-up between the valve and valve seat which will make the engine hard to start. |
| Service after use | Drain cooling water. | After stopping the engine, drain cooling water by opening the cocks of the cooling water pump and exhaust manifold. Complete drainage is obtained by turning the flywheel. In cold weather, close the Kingstone cock. | In cold weather, frozen water in the cylinder head will damage the engine. |

| | Treatment | Instruction to engine operator | Reason |
|---|---|---|---|
| Storing engine | Cleaning the engine. | While the engine is still warm, completely remove oil and dirt. | For better maintenance of engine. |
| | Change lube oil. | Change lube oil and turn the engine through few times. | For next use. Rust preventive treatment. |
| | Moving parts free from corrosion and dirt. | Wipe off oil and dirt. Apply oil to the following parts: 1. Link part of fuel pump. 2. Pinion shaft of cell motor. 3. Moving part of remote control device, shaft part of handles. Cover the engine with vinyle sheet, paper, or cloth for dust-proofing. | |
| | Occasionally turn the engine. | Turn the engine by hand once a month. | To rust-proof metal, piston, liner and rings. |
| | Store battery. | Disconnect battery leads and store in a dry place. Charge once a month. | |

## 2. Time of Periodic Checks

A periodic check is necessary to keep the engine in good condition at all times. The frequency of such checks may vary, depending upon engine use, conditions of use, quality of oil used, and methods of operating the engine. It is difficult to specify the required frequency of periodic checks and service. Therefore, only general explanations will be given here. The relationship between the details of such checks and time is as follows:

## 2-1 Table of perodic checks

| Items | Contents / Operating hours | Daily | Every 50 hours | Every 250 hours | Every 500 hours | 1 yr or 1500 hours | Every 2000 hours | Every 3000 hours |
|---|---|---|---|---|---|---|---|---|
| Fuel | Check fuel level. Replenish. | O | | | | | | |
| | Remove condensation from fuel tank. | O (Before replenishment) | | | | | | |
| | Remove condensation in fuel strainer. | | O | | | | | |
| | Clean and overhaul fuel strainer. | | | O | | | | |
| Engine oil | Check oil level. Replenish. | O | | | | | | |
| | Remove condensation in oil strainer. | | O | | | | | |
| | Disassemble and clean oil strainer. | | | O | | | | |
| | Change oil. | | | O | (The first change be made 50 hours after starting of the engine newly installed.) | | | |
| Cooling water pump, etc. | Check cooling water circulation. | O | | | | | | |
| | Clean thermostat. | | | O | | | | |
| | Check and tighten gland packing. | When excessive leak is observed. | | | | | | |
| | Check and replace protective zinc. | | | | O | | | |
| | Overhaul check of major components. | | | | | O | | |
| Governor | Overhaul check of major components. | | | | | | O | |
| | Check and adjust governor linkage. | | | O | | | | |
| Fuel injection pump | Check injection timing. | | | | O | | | |
| | Check delivery valve. | | | | O | | | |
| | Overhaul check of major components. | | | | | | O | |
| Fuel injection valve | Check spray condition. | | | | O | | | |
| | Check and adjust injection pressure. | | | | O | | | |
| | Overhaul cleaning of fuel strainer and injection valve. | | | | O | | | |
| Cylinder head | Retighten head bolts. | 50 hours after trial operation of new or reconditioned engine. | | | | | | |
| | Adjust intake and exhaust valve clearances. | | | | O | | | |
| | Grind intake and exhaust valves. | | | | | O | | |
| | Check rocker arms and valve guides. | | | | | O | | |
| | Clean combustion and pre-combustion chambers. | | | | | O | | |

| Items | Contents | Operating hours / Daily | Every 50 hours | Every 250 hours | Every 500 hours | 1 yr or 1500 hours | Every 2000 hours | Every 3000 hours |
|---|---|---|---|---|---|---|---|---|
| Piston | Overhaul, clean, and check rings. | | | | | O | | |
| Connecting rod | Check bearings, bolts, and torque. | | | | | O | | |
| Main bearings | Check bearings and bolts. | | | | | | | O |
| Crank shaft | Measure and check pin and journal diameters. | | | | | | | O |
| | Measure and check crank arm deflection. | | | | | O | | |
| Engine exterior | Check miscellaneous bolts, nuts, and for oil leaks. | O | | | | | | |
| All engine piping | Check for leaks. | O | | | | | | |
| Clutch | Overhaul, check, and recondition moving parts. | | | | | | | O |

## 2-2 Every 50 hours

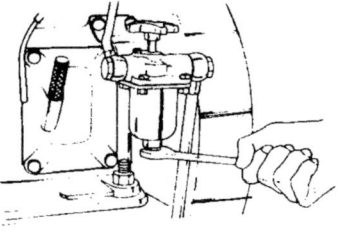

(1) **To remove fuel strainer drain:**

① Close the fuel tank stopcock.
② Remove the drain plug from the bottom of the fuel strainer, as illustrated and drain the fuel strainer.
③ Replace the drain plug and firmly tighten.
④ Open the fuel tank stopcock and vent air.

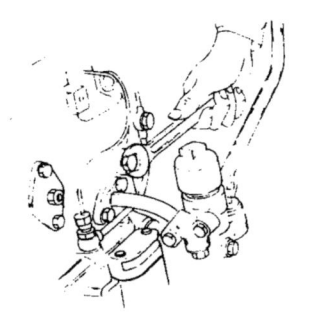

(2) **To remove lube oil strainer drain:**

① Remove the drain plug from the side of the lube oil strainer, as illustrated, drain lube oil and take out the drain.
② Replace the drain plug and firmly tighten.

## 2-3 Every 250 hours

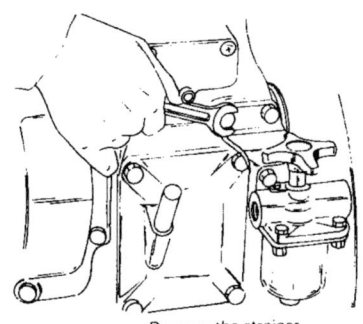

Remove the strainer

(1) **To clean the fuel strainer:**

① Close the fuel tank stopcock.
② Disconnect the two pipes on the side of the fuel strainer.
③ Remove the fuel strainer mounting bolts, as illustrated.
④ Loosen the four strainer cover bolts and carefully remove the strainer element.
⑤ Clean the strainer element by rinsing with light oil.
⑥ Thoroughly clean the strainer housing inside with light oil.
⑦ Following cleaning, reassemble the fuel strainer by reversing the disassembly procedure and remount on the engine.
⑧ After reassembly, vent air.

(2) **To change lube oil:**

Lube oil can be easily changed, just after operation, while the engine is still warm, since the oil will flow freely. Remove any lubricating oil in the engine by using the hand operated lube oil evacuation pump.

① Remove lube oil from the crank case by setting the evacuation pump valve as shown in the figure.

② Next, remove clutch case lube oil by turning the evacuation pump valve to the position shown in the figure.

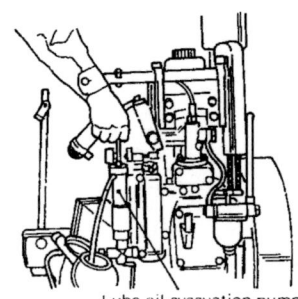
Lube oil evacuation pump

(3) **To disassemble and clean the lube oil strainer:**

① Loosen the drain plug, drain the lube oil, and take out the drain.
② Disconnect pipes as shown, loosen the three strainer cover bolts and carefully remove the strainer element.
③ Clean the strainer element by rinsing with light oil and then dry.
④ Use a sponge to wipe off oil inside the strainer housing.
⑤ After cleaning, reassemble the lube oil strainer and remount on the engine.

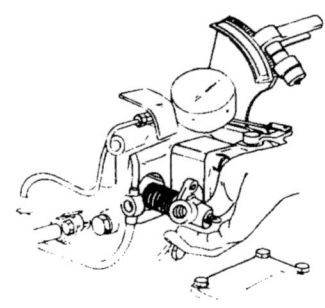

## 2-4 Every 500 hours

(1) **Adjustment of suction and exhaust valve clearances.**

When the engine is cold and the exhaust valves are completely closed (top dead center in the compression stroke), the clearance between the rocker arms and valve heads should be adjusted to 0.15 mm by using the supplied thickness gauge.

① Position the piston in the top dead center of the compression stroke (the top dead center of fuel injection).
② Loosen the rocker arm lock nut and adjust with the thickness gauge, while turning the valve head adjusting screw.
③ After adjustment, fix the adjusting screw position with the lock nut.

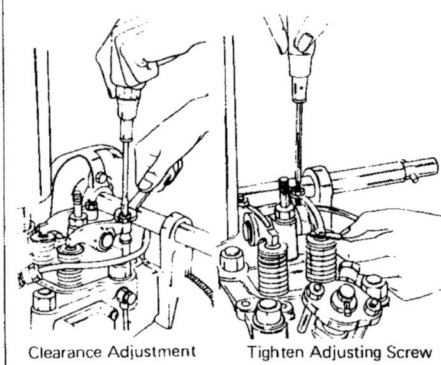
Clearance Adjustment     Tighten Adjusting Screw

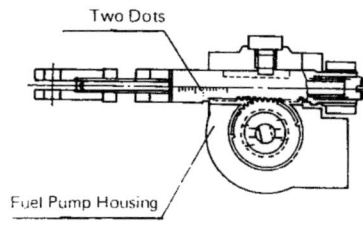

Two Dots

Fuel Pump Housing

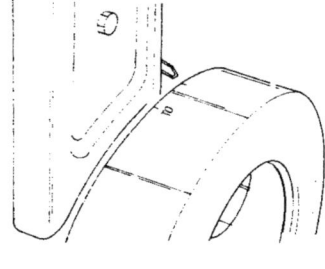

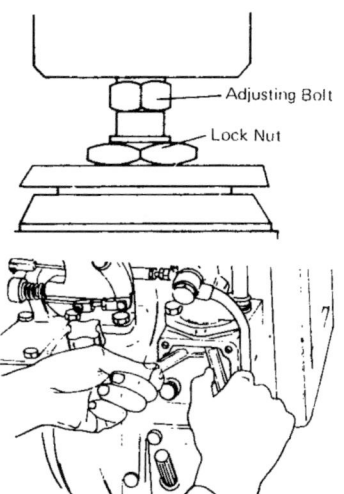

Adjusting Bolt

Lock Nut

**(2) To check fuel injection timing:**

If fuel injection timing is not correct engine power will be less than maximum.

① With the engine in position to start compression, take the high pressure fuel pipes off the fuel injection pump.

② Align the two dots marked on the rack with the edge of the pump housing.

③ While watching the fuel oil level in the outlet port of the fuel injection pump delivery valve spring holder ---

④ Set the decompression handle in the no-compression position and slowly turn the fly wheel in the running direction.

⑤ Stop the fly wheel the moment the oil level begins to change ---

⑥ And note the scale reading.

⑦ There is a relative scale of 12 units stamped on the fly wheel before top center. The relative degree before top dead center can be read from this. The timing is set correctly when the pointer falls on the point 12 units before top dead center. If this is not the case refer to (3) "Adjustment of fuel injection timing."

**(3) Adjustment of fuel injection timing**

After checking (2) above, if adjustment is necessary use the following procedure to make adjustment:

① Open the square in the lower portion of the fuel injection pump.

② Loosen the lock nut and adjust timing by turning the adjusting bolt. Screwing the bolt in (moving the spanner from right to left) will set the injection timing back (the scale on the fly wheel moves closer to top dead center) and the timing can be set forward by screwing the adjusting bolt out.

③ Temporarily tighten the lock nut and recheck timing to make sure it is correct.

④ After adjustment, tighten the lock nut firmly to prevent the adjusting bolt from becoming loose.

(4) Inspection and Servicing of the fuel injection valve

① To clean the fuel strainer:
Ⓐ Disconnect the high pressure fuel pipes and remove the fuel injection valve.
Ⓑ While holding the fuel injection valve with a vise carefully remove the fuel strainer barrel.
Ⓒ After removing the fuel strainer, as illustrated, wash out thoroughly with a light cleaning oil.
Ⓓ After cleaning, replace the fuel strainer in the fuel injection valve and reassemble the fuel injection system.

② To remove carbon from the spray nozzle: Carefully remove carbon deposits from the spray nozzle with a knife or hack saw blade, taking care not to damage the nozzle.

③ Injection pressure inspection:
Ⓐ Connect the nozzle tester to the fuel injection valve.
Ⓑ Pump the handle of the nozzle tester at a rate of 60 ~ 100 times per minute.
Ⓒ Read the pressure gauge just when the pointer, after a gradual rise, suddenly drops.
Ⓓ if this inspection reveals that the injection pressure has deviated from 160 kg/cm$^2$, refer to the next section ④ to readjustment injection pressure.

④ To adjust injection pressure:
Ⓐ Remove the fuel injection valve box nut.
Ⓑ Adjust the injection pressure by varying the number of pressure controlling plates inside (one injection controlling plate of 0.1 mm thickness changes the pressure about 10 kg/cm$^2$).
Ⓒ Tighten up the box nut and repeat the injection pressure inspection procedure in ③.

Box nut

Pressure controlling plate

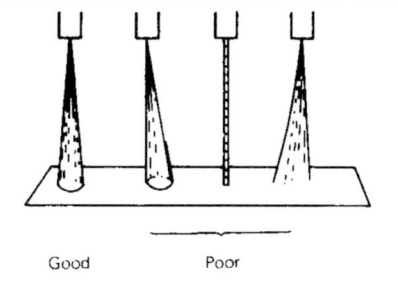

Good   Poor

⑤ To check injection:
Inspect spray formation by using the procedure of section ③.
Note: If the nozzle does not produce a conical spray adjustment or replacement will be necessary.
Ask your local Yanmar agent or dealer about adjustment or replacement.

Fuel Injection Pump
When the fuel injection pump is to be disassembled or reassembled, handle the parts with extra care so as not to damage or leave any dust on the parts.

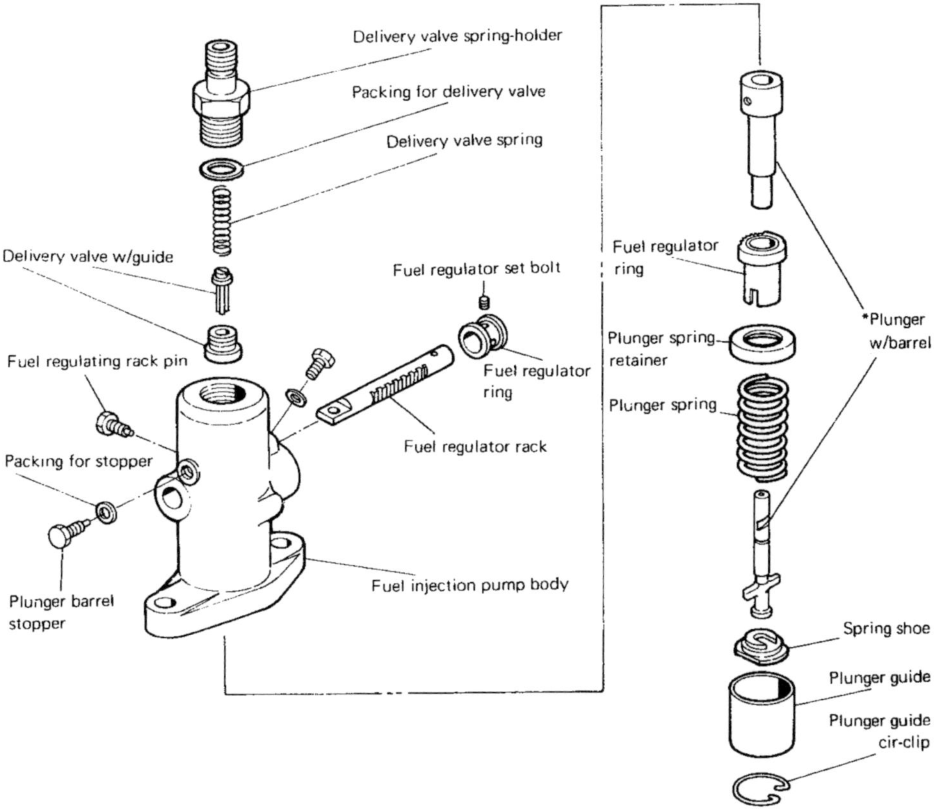

- Delivery valve spring-holder
- Packing for delivery valve
- Delivery valve spring
- Delivery valve w/guide
- Fuel regulator set bolt
- Fuel regulating rack pin
- Fuel regulator ring
- Packing for stopper
- Fuel regulator rack
- Plunger barrel stopper
- Fuel injection pump body
- Fuel regulator ring
- Plunger spring retainer
- Plunger spring
- *Plunger w/barrel
- Spring shoe
- Plunger guide
- Plunger guide cir-clip

*MARK: NOT SOLD SEPARATELY

- Insert the fuel regulator ring.
  Be sure to match cut mark of fuel reg. rack with the punch mark on the fuel regulator. (Refer to the Figure at right.)

- Insert the plunger.
  The correct plunger direction is attained by matching the O-point mark on the plunger side and the cut mark on the fuel regulator ring side.

- Insert the plunger spring holder, plunger spring, the plunger spring shoe, the plunger guide, and set the plunger guide lock ring.

- Place the fuel pump body upright.

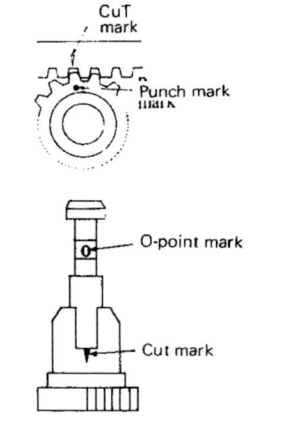

- **Fuel Injection Valve**
  The fuel injection valve of the Model SKE engine is designed to atomize the fuel delivered under high pressure from the fuel pump so that combustion takes place more easily. A major cause of poor engine performance is incomplete fuel atomization.
  A nozzle valve is used to insure complete atomization, while a pressure regulator maintains fuel injection at a constant pressure. Precise machining was required in the manufacture of this nozzle, therefore insure the nozzle does not incur any scratches or accumulation of dust during handling.

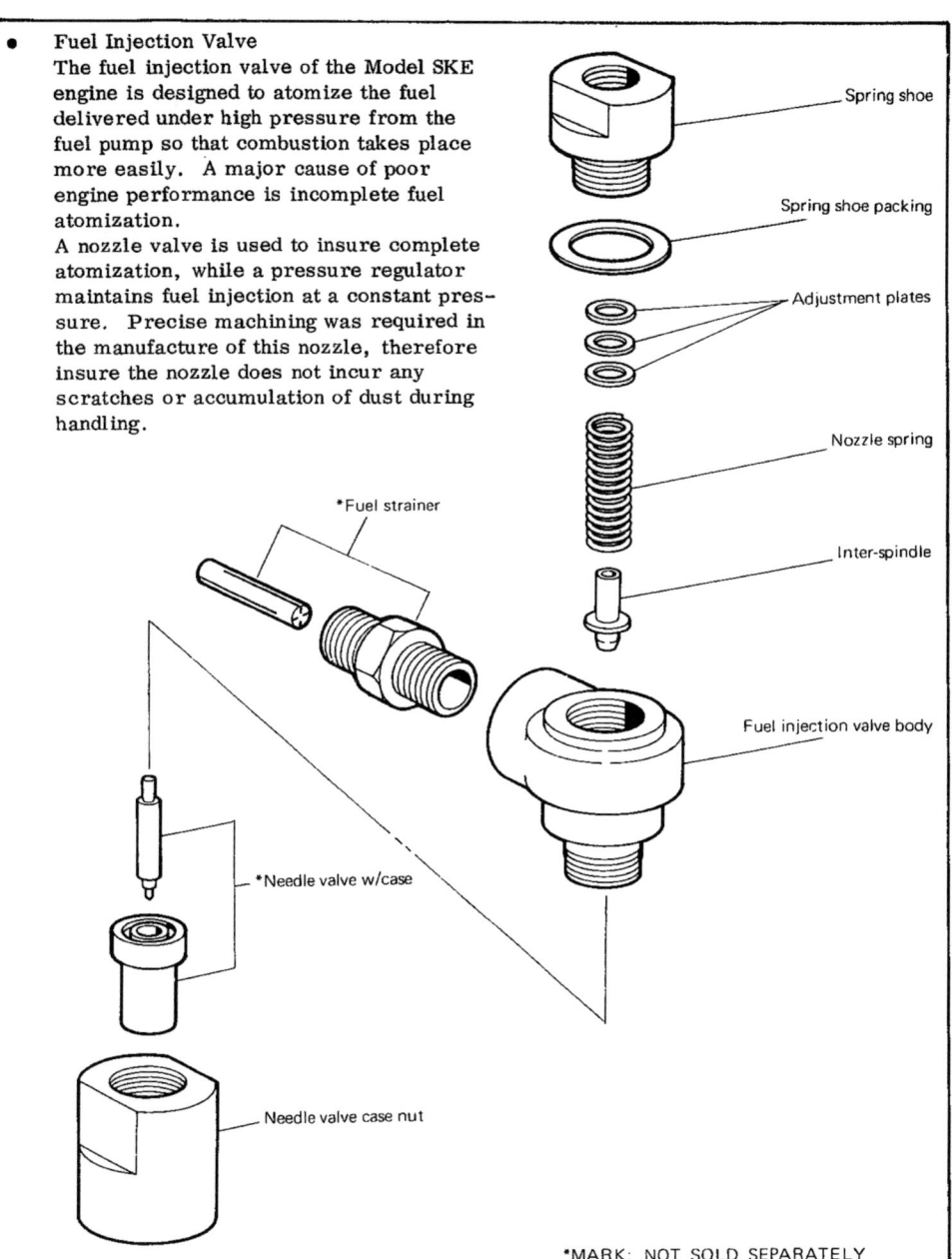

*MARK: NOT SOLD SEPARATELY

**(5) Inspection and replacement of proterctive zinc**

① A protective zinc strip is mounted on the cooling water pump side of the cylinder to prevent electrolytic corrosion.
  Ⓐ Remove tne fitting flange bolts and take off the flange with the zinc strip attached.
  Ⓑ If half of the zinc strip has corroded removing scale. replace it with a new one.

② To replace the protective zinc strip:
  Ⓐ Loosen the nut holding the protective zinc strip and take the strip off the flange.
  Ⓑ Use a knife or emery cloth to clean the flange surface.
  Ⓒ Firmly attach the new zinc strip to the flange.
  Ⓓ Replace the fitting flange on the side of the cylinder.

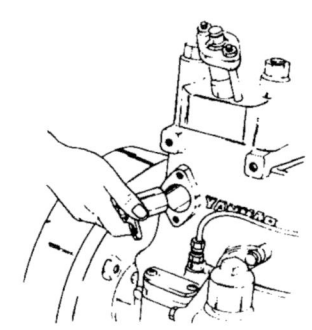

**(6) To remove the cylinder head:**

① Open the cooling water pump drain cock and drain the water from the cylinder head and jacket.
② Take off the bonnet and remove the cooling water outlet bend.
③ Disconnect the rocker arm lubricating pipe.
④ Disconnect the high pressure fuel pipes and remove the fuel injection valve.
⑤ Remove the air intake pipe.
⑥ Take off the chain guard and remove the starting shaft support.
⑦ Remove the exhaust bend.
⑧ Take off the rocker arm assembly and remove the push rods.
⑨ Loosen the cylinder head bolts and remove the cylinder head.

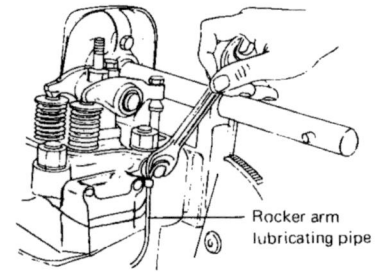

Rocker arm lubricating pipe

**(7) To remove suction and exhaust valves:**

① Place the cylinder head in such a way that the combustion surface points downward.

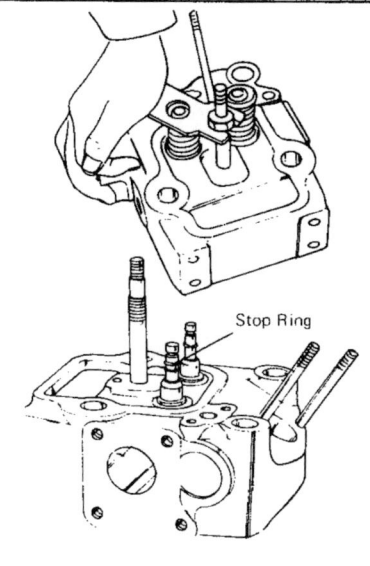

Stop Ring

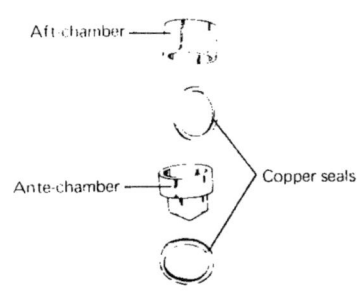

Aft-chamber

Ante-chamber — Copper seals

② Place a nut on the fitting bolt of the rocker arm shaft support and take out the stops by pressing down the valve spring as shown (Do not mix up the stops and spring retainers of the suction side and exhaust side).
③ Remove the valve springs and valve spring retainers.
④ Use pliers to remove the stop ring shown in the diagram.

(8) To remove and clean the pre-combustion chamber:

① Use your hands to remove the pre-combustion aft-chamber.
② Use a copper or wooden rod and hammer to remove the pre-combustion ante-chamber.
③ Thoroughly clean the inside of the injection nozzle.

Notes: Ⓐ Check the copper seals carefully, and if defective replace with a new one. Compressed air leaks will result if the seals are defective.
Ⓑ Anneal the copper seals before installing.

(9) To inspect and clean the cylinder head:

① Thoroughly clean the combustion surface by removing any deposited carbon with a knife or emery cloth.
② To clean the upper side of the cylinder head:
  Ⓐ Clean the inside of the suction and exhaust valve guides with light oil.
  Ⓑ Wash off any sludge and dirt adhering to the rocker arm chamber with light oil.
  Ⓒ Completely clean the valve push rod "O" ring grooves with a knife.

(10) To lap the suction and exhaust valves:

① Apply a lubricating oil to the side of the valve stem and a fine lapping powder to the valve seat and assemble the valve in the cylinder head.
② Lap the valve until a good flush contact is achieved, by rotating the valve and tapping it at the same time with a lapping tool as shown.
Note: Apply the lapping powder to the valve seat only and do not over apply.
③ When good contact is made, remove the lapping powder and repeat the lapping procedure above using oil in place of the lapping powder.
④ After lapping is finished, clean the valve and guide with light oil and then coat with lube oil.
Note: Be careful not to mix up the suction valve and exhaust valves while disassembled, because they are of different compositions.

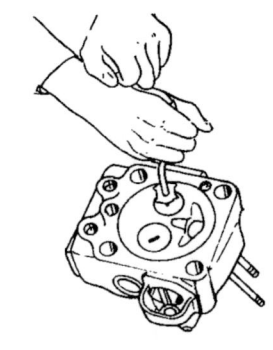

(11) To assemble the suction and exhaust valves:

① Coat the valve stem and seat with lube oil and then insert the valve stem into the valve guide.
② Reassemble the valve springs, valve spring retainers and the stops in the proper order.

(12) To install the cylinder head:

① If the copper cylinder head gasket has been removed, anneal before installing.
② Put new "O" rings in the cooling water connecting pipe and valve push rod covers.
③ Install the cylinder head and watch the "O" ring fit.
④ Attach the cylinder head clamping nuts and tighten them in a diagonal sequence to insure even pressure all around.
⑤ Insert the valve push rods.
⑥ Fit the exhaust bend.
⑦ Reconnect the rocker arm lubrication pipes.
⑧ Fit the chain on the sprockets, stretch the chain tight but allowing the starting shaft to operate when the shaft is turned counter-clockwise and then clamp the starting shaft

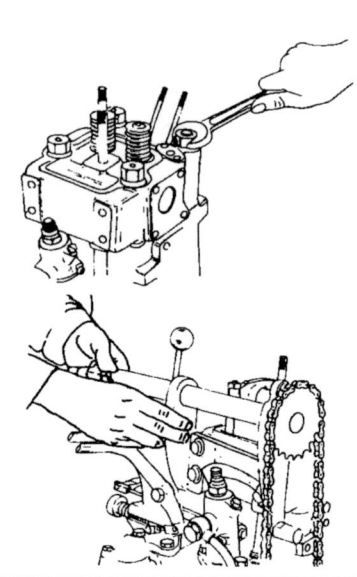

— 27 —

support. After installation of the chain make sure the shaft rotates smoothly in the counter-clockwise direction.
⑨ Reconnect the rocker arm shaft mount.
⑩ Replace the air intake pipe.
⑪ Adjust the valve clearances by referring to section 8-3 ①.
⑫ Replace the bonnet and make sure the fly wheel rotates smoothly.

## 2-5 Every 1500 hours

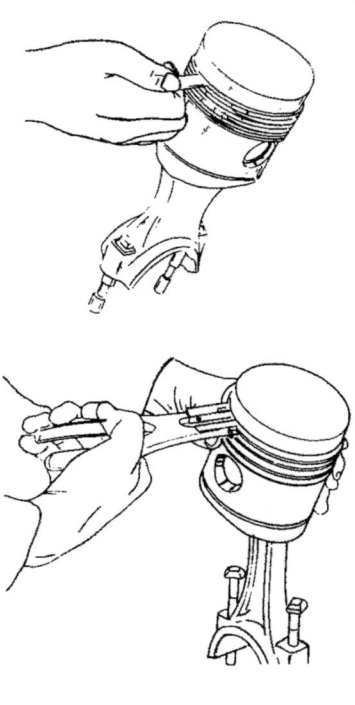

1) Piston removal.
    ① Remove the cylinder head by referring to paragraph 8-3 ⑥.
    ② Remove the cylinder side cover.
    ③ Pry up the lock washer locking lugs on the connecting rod bolts.
    ④ Remove the nuts from the connecting rod bolts.
    ⑤ Hold the bearing cap by hand and position the piston at top dead center (TDC), then remove the bearing cap.
    ⑥ Remove the piston by grasping the top and drawing it out, while pushing up on the connecting rod.

2) Cleaning the piston and piston rings.
    ① Remove carbon from the piston head with a hack-saw blade, or similar tool. Be sure not to score the surface.
    ② Remove carbon from the ring grooves by submerging the piston in solvent and slowly working the rings back and forth in the grooves.

3) Checking piston rings.
    Replace the rings if any of the following discrepancies are noted:
    ① Outer surface is worn unevenly, scored vertically, and/or signs of combustion leakage are present.
    ② Clearance between ring and ring groove exceeds 0.2 mm, when measured with a feeler gage, as illustrated.

4) Piston ring removal.
    ① Rings can be removed easily with the aid of a ring insertion tool, as illustrated.

② If a ring insertion tool is not available, loop very fine wire over the cut ends and spread slowly until the ring is clear of the groove.

Note: Be sure to note which side of the ring is the top and the order of installation before removal.

5) Cleaning ring grooves.

Thoroughly remove all carbon from the ring grooves, taking extra care not to score the groove.

6) Checking crank pin inserts.

The crank pin inserts have a long service life, even though they may be completely discolored by a uniform, brownish color. If heavy score marks are noted, or the insert has non-uniform discoloration, contact our agent or your service dealer on continued use of the insert.

7) Piston ring installation.

Installation of the piston rings is similar to disassembly, however, care must be exercised so that the ring is not broken when fitting it over the piston. Insure the correct side is "up" (stamp mark side), and that the order of installation is proper.

8) Piston assembly.
① After cleaning the crank pin, apply a light coat of oil.
② Position the crank pin at top dead center.
③ Apply a coat of oil to the crank pin insert and the piston.
④ Position the open end of the top piston ring parallel to the pin and the open ends of the remaining rings at right angles to each other, from the top down.
⑤ Insert the connecting rod in the cylinder, with the " 🎌 " mark on the flywheel side.
⑥ With the aid of the piston insertion tool, insert the piston in the cylinder, as illustrated.
⑦ Align the scribe mark on the large end of the connecting rod with the mark on the bearing cap and clamp the cap.
⑧ Use new lock washers and tighten the lock nuts on both connecting rods in an alternate manner until they are uniformly tight.

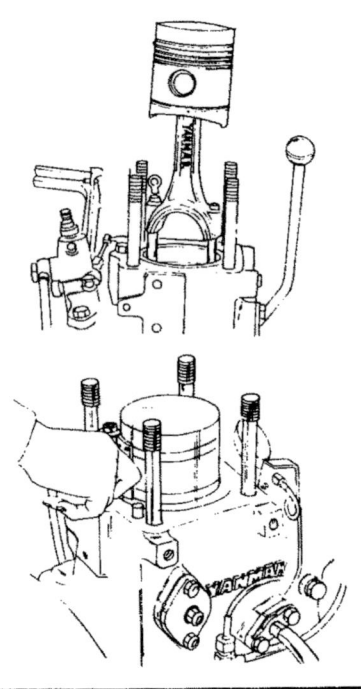

⑨ Bend the lugs on the lock washers down.
⑩ Turn the flywheel through by hand and insure rotation is smooth.
⑪ Re-assemble the cylinder head, referring to paragraph 8-3 (12).

**PISTON & CONNECTING ROD**

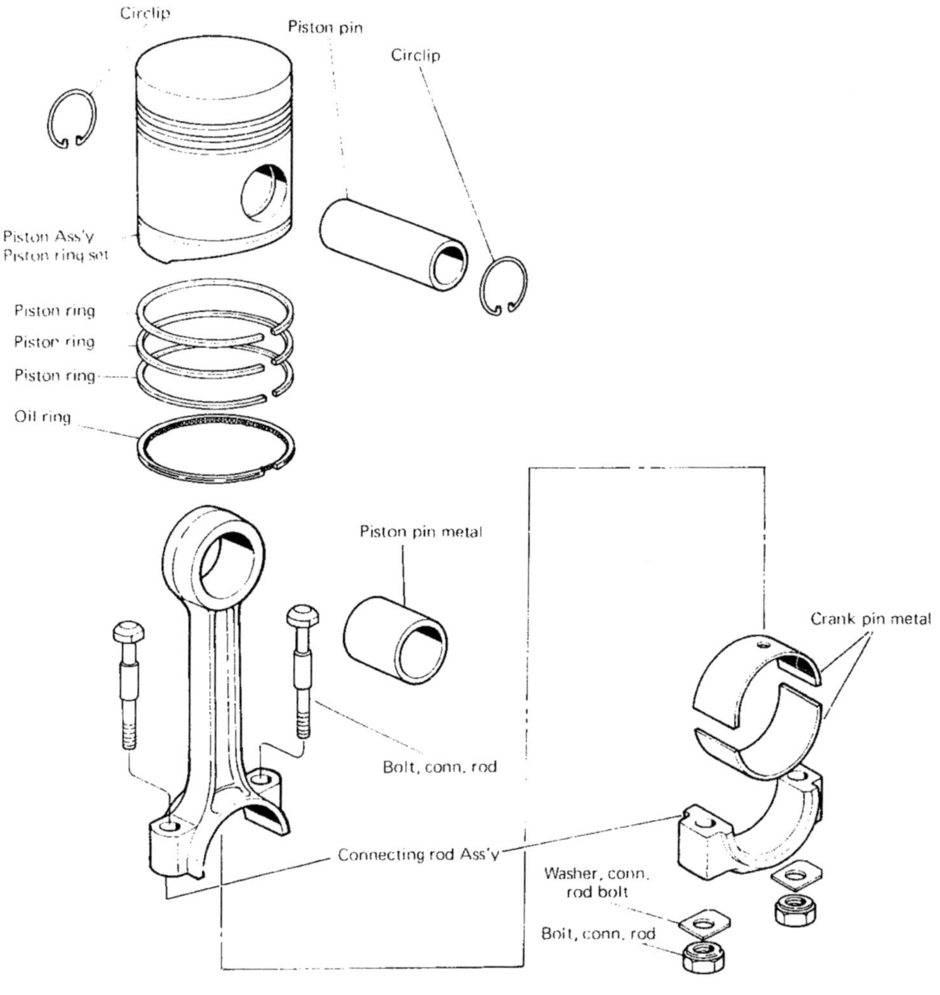

## 2-6 Other time interval checks

1) **Re-torquing cylinder head bolts.**
   ① Always re-torque the cylinder head bolts 50 operational hours after initial operation, and after overhauling the cylinder head.

2) **Checking and servicing water pump gland packing.**
   Check and retighten the water pump gland packing if excessive leaks are noted. (Refer to paragraph 5-3 (3))
   If the packing cannot be tightened sufficiently to stop such leakage, install additional packing or replace the old packing. Installation of additional packing is accomplished as follows, however, contact our agent or your nearest service dealer prior to commencing such work.

   ① Loosen the packing gland bolts and move the gland toward the engine.
   ② Insert the additional packing, pressing it in place evenly with a screwdriver. Re-position the gland so that it completely covers the packing.
   ③ Lightly tighten the packing gland bolts.
   ④ Start the engine and alternately tighten the gland bolts until all leakage stops.

3) **Operation and adjustment of clutch**
   ① Operation
   Clutch service life depends primarily on the manner in which it is operated during routine operations. When shifting from ahead to astern, or vice-versa, always reduce engine speed with the regulating handle. Momentarily position the handle to the neutral position before shifting to ahead or astern. Increase engine speed only after the clutch is fully engaged. Never operate the clutch handle rapidly with the engine at high speed when shifting from one position to another. Such operations will damage the clutch.

   ② Adjustment.
   Adjustment of this clutch is not necessary, even after a long period of service. Contact our agent or your local service dealer when replacing the friction plate, or when any other discrepancies occur.

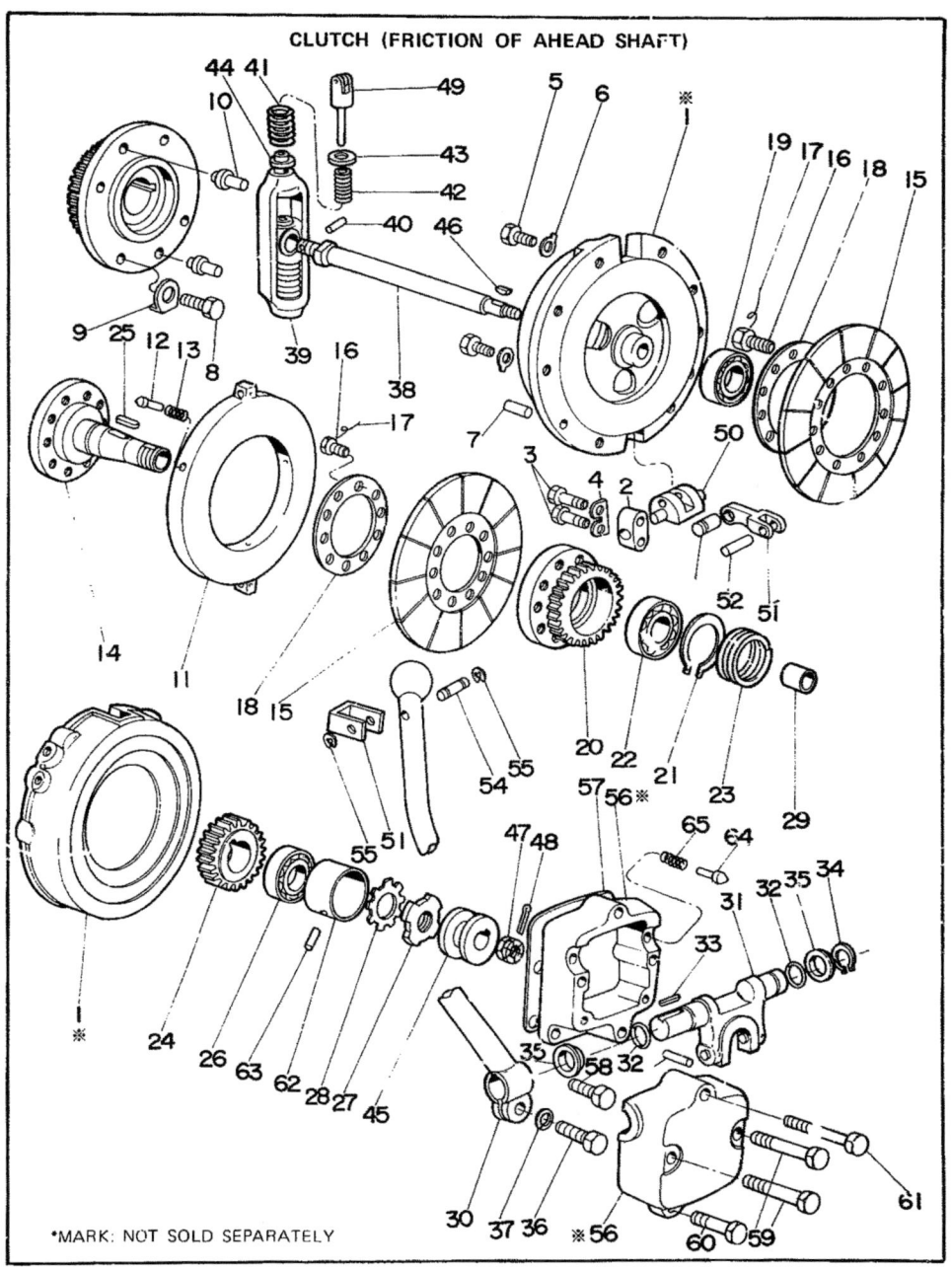

| Item | Part name | Item | Part name | Item | Part name |
|---|---|---|---|---|---|
| 1 | Disc housing ass'y | 23 | Spring | 45 | Shifter |
| 2 | Piece, v-lever | 24 | Pinion, Z = 23<br>Pinion, Z = 19 | 46 | Woodruff key 4 X 13 |
| 3 | Bolt | 25 | Feather key 7 x 26 | 47 | Nut M12 |
| 4 | Washer | 26 | Ball bearing 6205 | 48 | Cotter pin 3 $\phi$ x 25 |
| 5 | Hex. bolt M8 x 20 | 27 | Lock nut | 49 | Push rod W/Roller |
| 6 | Lock washer | 28 | Washer | 50 | V-lever |
| 7 | Parallel pin 8 $\phi$ x 18 | 29 | Bush | 51 | Link |
| 8 | Hex. bolt M10 x 35 | 30 | Lever | 52 | Pin |
| 9 | Lock washer | 31 | Fork lever | 53 | Joint |
| 10 | Pin W Collar | 32 | O-ring P18 | 54 | Pin |
| 11 | Friction plate | 33 | Feather key 5 x 18 | 55 | Circlip 7 |
| 12 | Claw | 34 | Circlip 18 | 56 | Rear case ass'y, ahead shaft |
| 13 | Spring, claw | 35 | Stopper, o-ring | 57 | Packing, rear case |
| 14 | Ahead shaft | 36 | Hex. bolt M10 x 25 | 58 | Hex. bolt M8 x 20 |
| 15 | Friction disc ass'y | 37 | Spring washer 10<br>Shaft ass'y | 59 | Hex. bolt M8 x 90 |
| 16 | Hex. bolt M8 x 12 | 38 | Shaft, shifting | 60 | Hex. bolt M8 x 36 |
| 17 | Wire (1.0) | 39 | Case | 61 | Hex. bolt M8 x 55 |
| 18 | Plate, disk | 40 | Taper pin 4 $\phi$ x 40 | 62 | Spacer, pinion |
| 19 | Ball bearing DD6205 | 41 | Spring (outside) | 63 | Parallel pin 6 $\phi$ x 8 |
| 20 | Shaft, reversing | 42 | Spring (inside) | 64 | Claw |
| 21 | Circlip 55 | 43 | Retainer | 65 | Spring, claw |
| 22 | Ball bearing 6006 | 44 | Retainer | | |

## 3. Electric Wiring

### Model SKE Electrical Wiring Diagram (Electric start type)

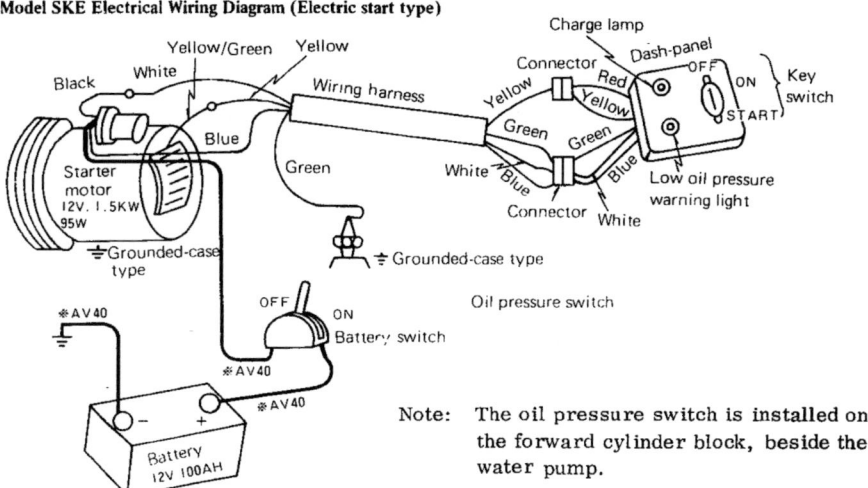

Note: The oil pressure switch is installed on the forward cylinder block, beside the water pump.

① Wiring precautions.
- Use the wire size specified in the wiring diagram for wires marked *
- Insure polarity is not reversed during wiring installation.
- Protect all terminals with an anti-corrosion coating.

② Operational precautions
- To maintain the battery at peak performance, check the level and specific gravity of the electrolyte monthly.
- Turn the battery switch OFF when charging the battery from another source.
- Check the starter drive belt for correct tension and damage monthly.
- DO NOT turn off the battery switch when the engine is running.

# ELECTRIC STARING DEVICE

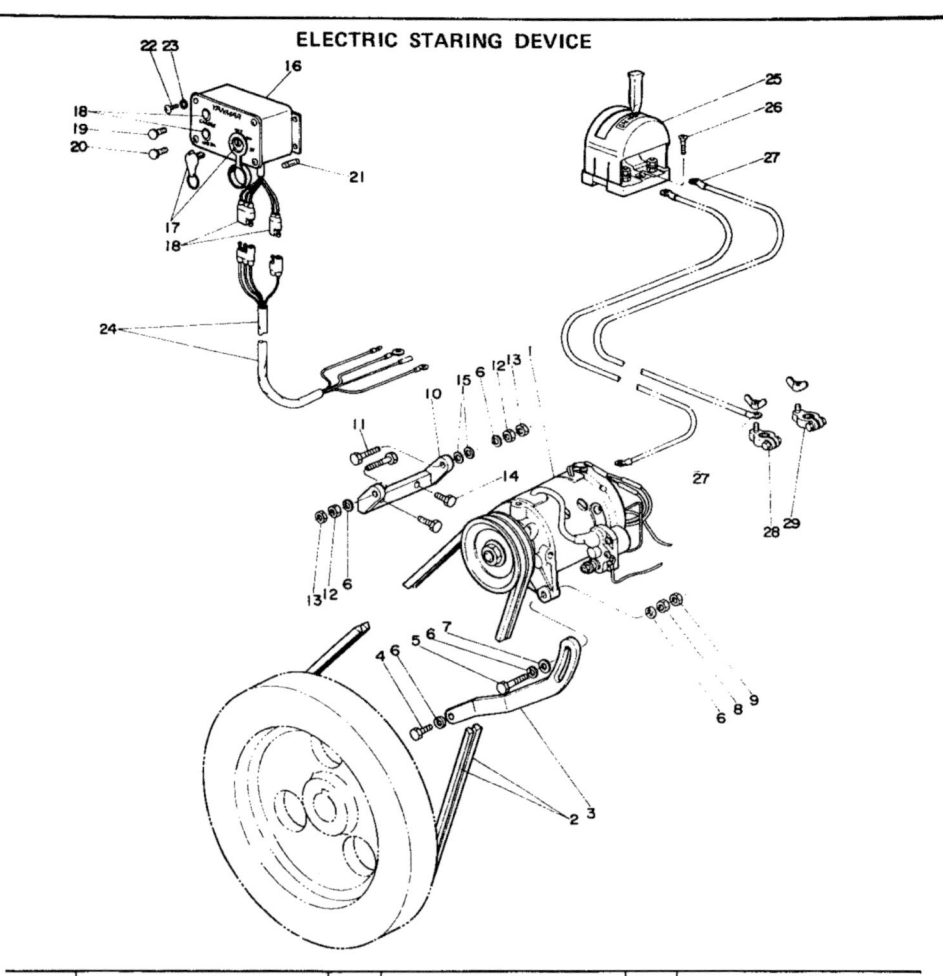

| Item | Part Name | Item | Part Nme | Item | Part Name |
|---|---|---|---|---|---|
| 1 | Starting dynamo | 11 | Hex. bolt M10 x 45 | 21 | Fuse 10A |
| 2 | V-belt HM-type | 12 | Nut M10 | 22 | Screw M4 x 8 |
| 3 | Adjuster, V-belt | 13 | Lock nut M10 | 23 | Plain washer 4 |
| 4 | Hex. bolt M10 x 32 | 14 | Hex. bolt M10 x 25 | 24 | Wire harness |
| 5 | Hex. bolt M10 x 45 | 15 | Shim, dynamo bracket | 25 | Switch, battery |
| 6 | Spring washer 10 | 16 | Dashboard | 26 | Screw M8 x 20 |
| 7 | Plain washer | 17 | Switch | 27 | Terminal BA608 |
| 8 | Nut M10 | 18 | Lamp ass'y | 28 | Terminal BE518 |
| 9 | Lock nut M10 | 19 | Lamp, charging-indicator | 29 | Terminal BE516 |
| 10 | Bracket, starting dynamo | 20 | Lamp, oil-indicator | | |

# V. Maintenance Standards for Main Components

When an engine is used over a long period of time, parts will wear. This not only reduces engine performance, but also results in engine problems unless the worn parts are replaced. A list containing maximum wear limits for main engine components follows at the end of this section. These limits of wear are estimated values which assure maximum engine performance, thus they are not absolute values by which component life is guaranteed. As indicated in the section on periodic checks and servicing, it is recommended that those parts which may require replacement before the next scheduled check be replaced during the current inspection. This procedure will reduce maintenance costs and lost operating time due to unscheduled maintenance.

### 1. Engine Disassembly Precautions

Prior to disassembling the engine, the following precautions should be observed:
1) A clean, dust-free workshop should be available for the disassembly.
2) Prepare a table or workbench on which the disassembled parts can be placed and covered to prevent damage or loss before reassembly.
3) A clean container full of cleaning solvent is required to clean the parts as they are removed.
4) Assemble the following tools:

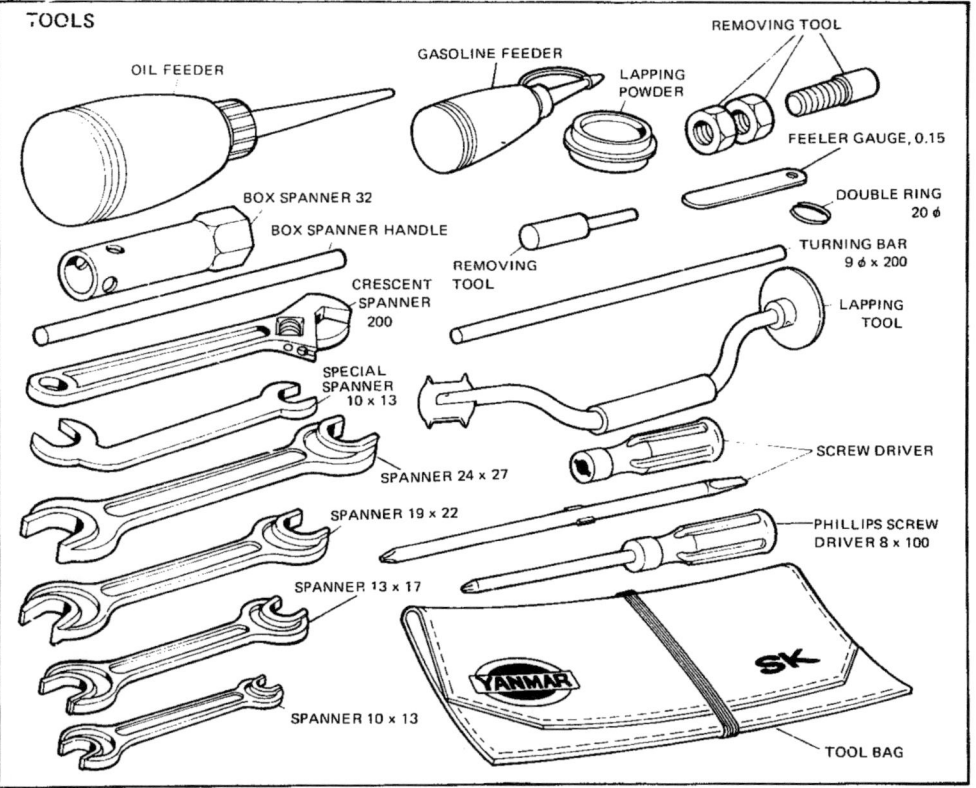

TOOLS

● Special tools (special order)
(1) Gear puller tools, complete
(2) Flywheel puller tools, complete
(3) Spline piece & free wheel puller tool, complete
(4) Gear box puller tool, complete
(5) Piston insertion tool
(6) Cylinder liner removal tool
(7) Suction/exhaust valve seat cutters, complete

● Measuring instruments:
(1) Vernier calipers
(2) Micrometer
(3) Cylinder gauge
(4) Feeler gauge
(5) Depth gauge
(6) Tachometer
(7) Torque wrench
(8) Fuel injection pump tester
(9) Fuel injection valve tester

● Other items to be prepared:
(1) White paint
(2) Sealing agent
(3) Red lead
(4) Fine lapping powder
(5) Chromium oxide

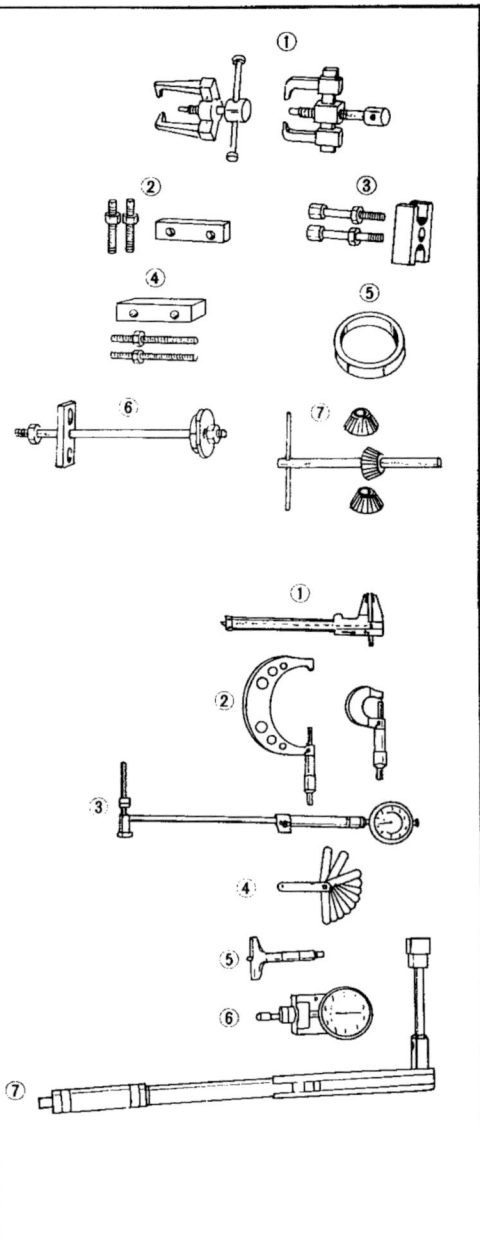

**General Precautions for Maintenance and Cleaning**

The following precautions should be observed during maintenance and cleaning:
(1) Make a good visual inspection of each part for carbon deposits and scoring. This practice will be very helpful in determing required maintenance.
(2) Be careful not to damage the parts when removing carbon deposits.
(3) Avoid using a wire brush or sandpaper for cleaning precision parts, such as the contact surfaces of suction and exhaust valves, the reciprocating surface of plungers, etc.
(4) Use only clean solvent for the final washing.
(5) Thoroughly clean the outside of the engine block and the inside of the crankcase at the time of disassembly. Prior to reassembly also clean those parts and locations that may be difficult to clean afterwards.
(6) Clean all oil holes subject to oil sludge settling and the inside of oil pipes thoroughly, not only with solvent but also with pressurized air.
(7) Clean all rusty surfaces with fine sandpaper and apply oil afterwards.
(8) Replace all scored parts.
(9) If scratches or small dents occur during disassembly, remove such marks or dents by rubbing with an oil-stone.
(10) After installing new parts, carefully inspect them for correct installation, contact, and clearances.

**Precautions for Disassembling the Engine**

The following precautions should be observed during disassembly of the engine:
(1) Disassemble the engine according to the given disassembly procedures.
(2) Do not disassemble any parts unnecessarily.
(3) Do not scratch or damage parts.
(4) Use only proper tools.
(5) Provide appropriate locks when disassembly work is difficult, since such parts as shafts tend to turn with their accessories.

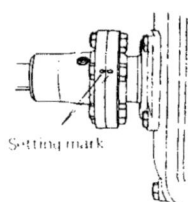

Thrust Shaft & Propeller Shaft

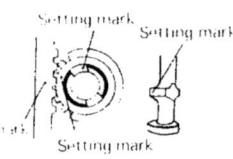

Pinion & Rack

(6) For removal of such parts as shafts, use appropriate brass or copper rod and doubling plates.
(7) Arrange the disassembled parts in order of removal.
(8) Confirm original positions by score marks. The following parts are provided with score marks:

Connecting rod large end, and its metal bushing, connecting rod large end and rod bolt: metal bushing and rod bolt nuts; crank journal metal bolts and nuts; camshaft gear and crank & gear; clutch box front cover and clutch box; friction plate support and clutch box sliding side cover; spline piece and friction plate: shaft couplings for thrust shaft and propeller or intermediate shaft: fuel control pinion and fuel adjusting rack of fuel injection pump; fuel control pinion and plunger of fuel injection pump.

(9) Make the most out of disassembly by cleaning those sections usually difficult to clean.
(10) Wash clean the disassembled parts and arrange in order.

## 2. Clearances and Tolerances of Main Components

### (1) Maximum Wear Limits

When the engine used over a long period of time, each part will wear, reducing performance or causing breakage of the crank shaft and piston pin, unless such defective parts are replaced. Figures to be referred to for replacement of parts are given in the following table. In practical operations, however, no trouble will occur immediately when wear of some parts exceeds these figures.
Time should always be considered in judging wear of parts. Therefore, care must be taken to avoid customer misunderstanding when using the figures in this table.

### (2) Clearances & Tolerances

| Part Name | | | | Nominal size | Difference in size | Standard Clearance of Ass'y | Maximum Allowable Clearance | Limits of Use | Corrective Measures |
|---|---|---|---|---|---|---|---|---|---|
| Cylinder liner | Inner dia. | | | 92 φ | +0.030 / 0 | | | Up to wearing of chrome plating | Change liner |
| | Lug of rubber packing | | | | | One side 0.52~0.75 | | | Change when changing liner |
| Clearance between piston and cylinder liner | Outer dia. of piston | Top | | 92 φ | −0.505 / −0.535 | | | | |
| | | Skirt | | 92 φ | 0.130 / 0.160 | | | 0.3 | Change piston |
| | Inner dia. of liner | | | | +0.030 / 0 | 0.13~0.19 | | | |
| Compression clearance | | | | 1.1 | +0.1 | 1.0~1.2 | | | |
| Piston ring | Contact clearance (against standard dia). | Inside of liner | Pressure ring | | | 0.3~0.5 | | 1.5 | Change rings |
| | | | Oil scraping ring | | | 0.3~0.5 | | 1.5 | Change rings |
| | | Free condition | Pressure ring No. 1 | | | Approx. 11.5 | | | |
| | | | Pressure ring No. 2,3 | | | Approx. 11.5 | | | |
| | | | Oil scraping ring | | | Appox. 11.5 | | | |
| | Clearance between piston ring and ring groove | Pressure ring | Width of ring No. 1 | 3.5 | −0.01 | 0.02~0.055 | 0.2 | 0.10 / +0.15 | Change rings |
| | | | Width of ring No. 2,3 | 2.5 | −0.03 | | | | |
| | | | Width of groove No. 1 | 3.5 | +0.025 | | | | |
| | | | Width of groove No. 2,3 | 2.5 | +0.010 | | | | |
| | | Oil ring | Width of ring | 4.5 | 0.01 / −0.03 | 0.02~0.055 | 0.2 | 0.10 / +0.15 | Change rings |
| | | | Width of groove | | +0.025 / +0.010 | | | | |
| Piston pin | Inner dia. of piston boss | | | 32 φ | −0.004 / −0.020 | Clearance (Tightening) 0.02~0.009 | | −0.07 | Change |
| | Outer dia. of piston pin | | | 32 φ | 0 / −0.013 | | | | Change |

| Part Name | | | | Nominal size | Difference in size | Standard Clearance of Ass'y | Maximum Allowable Clearance | Limits of Use | Corrective Measures |
|---|---|---|---|---|---|---|---|---|---|
| Piston pin | Inner dia. of piston bush | | | 32 φ | +0.050<br>+0.030 | Clearance<br>0.03 – 0.063 | 0.15 | | Change |
| Crank shaft | Crank pin | Outer dia. of crank pin | | 56 φ | -0.040<br>-0.060 | 0.105 | 0.15 | -0.7 | When uneven wear of pin exceeds 0.06 mm, regrind the pin and use undersized insert. (size: -0.25,-0.5) |
| | | Inner dia. of bearing | | | +0.045<br>0 | | | | |
| | Journal | Dia. | Outer dia. of journal | 58 φ | 0.036<br>0.061 | 0.039 – 0.096 | 0.15 | 0.7 | When uneven wear of pin exceeds 0.06 mm, regrind the pin and use undersized insert. (size: -0.25,-0.5) |
| | | | Dia. of bearing | | +0.035<br>+0.018 | | | | |
| | | Side clearance | Width of journal | 99 | 0<br>0.05 | 0.13 – 0.25 | — | 0.5 | When the metal is worn beyond limits of use, use oversized insert. 0.1, 0.2. |
| | | | Standard width of bearing | | | | | | |
| Cam shaft | Dia. | Outer dia. of journal | | — | — | — | — | — | — |
| | | Inner dia. of bearing | | — | — | — | — | — | — |
| | Width | Standard width of journal | | — | — | — | — | — | — |
| | | Standard width of bearing | | — | — | — | — | — | — |
| | Height of cam for suc. & exh. valves | | | 38 | ±0.03 | — | — | -0.5 | Change |
| Suction & exh. valves | Clearance between valve rod & valve guide | Suc. | Valve rod outer dia. | 9 φ | -0.041<br>-0.051 | 0.041 – 0.066 | 0.25 | -0.15 | Change valve or valve guide |
| | | | Valve guide inner dia. | | +0.015<br>0 | | | | |
| | | Exh. | Valve rod outer dia. | 9 φ | -0.041<br>-0.055 | 0.041 – 0.070 | 0.20 | 0.15 | |
| | | | Valve guide inner dia. | | +0.015<br>0 | | | | |
| | Valve seat | Angle | | 90° | — | — | — | — | — |
| | | Width | | 2·16 | — | — | — | 2·6 | — |
| | | Sink | | 1·25 | | — | — | 2·5 | Change valve seat (exhaust side) |
| | Top Clearance | Suction valve | | — | | 0.15 | — | 0.10 – 0.20 | — |
| | | Exhaust valve | | — | | 0.15 | — | 0.10 – 0.20 | — |

## 3. Exchange Standards for Wear of Main Parts

| | Specifications for Main Parts | | Calculation Basis for Wear Limits | Standard Size (unit-mm) | Limits of Measument |
|---|---|---|---|---|---|
| **Limit of Wear** | Inner dia. of cylinder liner | | 0.003D | 92 φ | +0.3 |
| | Outer dia. of piston skirt | | 0.0025d | 92 φ | −0.25 |
| | Outer dia. of piston pin | | 0.005d | 32 φ | −0.19 |
| | Inner dia. of piston pin insert | | 0.005D | 32 φ | +0.19 |
| | Outer dia. of crankshaft pin part | | 0.003d | 56 φ | +0.20 |
| | Outer dia. of crankshaft journal | | 0.003d | 58 φ | −0.20 |
| | Inner dia. of crank pin insert | | 0.004D | 56 φ | +0.28 |
| | Inner dia. of crank insert | | 0.004D | 58 φ | +0.28 |
| | No. 1 piston ring | Width | — | 3.5 | −0.20 |
| | | Thickness | 0.15t | 3.7 | −0.65 |
| | No. 2 − 3 piston ring | Width | — | 2.5 | −0.20 |
| | | Thickness | 0.15t | 3.7 | −0.65 |
| | Oil ring (without expansion ring) | Width | — | 4.5 | −0.20 |
| | | Thickness | 0.15t | 3.2 | −0.65 |
| | Outer dia. cam shaft journal | | 0.003d | 30 φ<br>25 φ | −0.15<br>−0.10 |
| | Height of cam shaft cam | | — | 38 | −0.40 |
| **Clearance** | Clearance between piston ring and piston groove | | — | 0.037 | +0.40 |
| | Clearance between piston pin and bushing | | 0.0075d | 0.048 | +0.28 |
| | Clearance between crank pin and crank pin insert | | 0.0055d | 0.072 | +0.42 |
| | Clearance between crank journal and crank insert | | 0.0055d | 0.067 | +0.42 |

| Measured Part | Measuring Position | Remarks | Measuring Instrument |
|---|---|---|---|
| Inner dia. of Cylinder liner | | Measure in (a)(b) directions at * marked position. (* mark is positioned on No. 1 piston ring at upper dead center.) | Cylinder gauge |
| Outer dia. of piston skirt | | Measure in (a)(b) direction at * marked position of piston skirt. | Micrometer |
| Clearance between cylinder liner and piston | | Insert piston skirt into the upper part of cylinder liner (No. 1 piston ring position at top dead center) and measure clearance in the directions of crank shaft motion and at right angles to the crank shaft. | Feeler gauge |
| Outer dia. of piston pin | | Maximum wear measured in (a)(b) directions at central * marked position. | Micrometer |
| Inner dia. of piston pin insert | | Maximum wear dimensions, measure insert inner dia. in (a)(b) directions. | Cylinder gauge |
| Clearance between piston and piston pin insert | | Maximum clearance measured in horizontal and vertical directions. | Feeler gauge |
| Outer dia. of crankshaft journal and crank insert | | Maximum wear dimensions measured at * mark in (a)(b) directions. | Micrometer |

| Measured Part | Measuring Position | Remarks | Measuring Instrument |
|---|---|---|---|
| Inner dia. of crank inserts (handle side and flywheel side) | | Measure in horizontal and vertical directions at * marked position. | Cylinder gauge |
| Thickness & width of piston rings | Width / Thickness | | Micrometer |
| Width of ring groove | | | Use new piston ring as thickness gauge |
| Clearance between piston ring and ring groove | | Maximum clearance between ring and groove | Feeler gauge |
| Simple method of measuring inner dia. of cylinder liner or thickness of piston ring | Use a new part for either the cylinder liner or piston ring (Cylinder liner, A, Piston ring) | Measure piston ring fitting dimension. Calculation of wear in inner dia. direction. $$\frac{A - 0.3}{3.14} = \text{wear}$$ Here, if the cylinder liner is new, it is the doubled amount of wear in thickness of ring. If a new ring is used, it is the amount of wear in inner dia. of cylinder liner. | Feeler gauge |

| Measured Part | Measuring Position | Remarks | Measuring Instrument |
|---|---|---|---|
| Height of cam on cam shaft | Height | Maximum height of cam | Micrometer |

## 4. Specified Tightening Torque for Major Parts

Major bolts and nuts of the engine should be tightened to the specified torque.

| Parts | Torque |
|---|---|
| Connecting rod bolts & nuts | 6.6 kg-m |
| Cylinder head bolts | 10 kg-m |
| Flywheel retaining nut | 24 kg-m |
| Balance weight retaining bolt | 6 kg-m |

Engine troubles must be detected in the early stages and defective parts repaired in order to prevent further damage. Trouble symptoms must be found quickly by heating, seeing, smelling, touching, or operator reports. Once the location of the troble has been determined, it should be decided what kind of repair is required. To do this properly, it is necessary to follow logical troubleshooting procedures. In order to readily find and repair malfunctions, the operator is required to completely understand each system and its function. If trouble is caused by operator misuse, he must be instructed so that the problem does not reoccur. The main engine problems, causes, and corrective measures are as follows.

1. Engine Problems, Causes, and Corrective Measures

(1) When engine does not start, or is difficult to start:

Causes

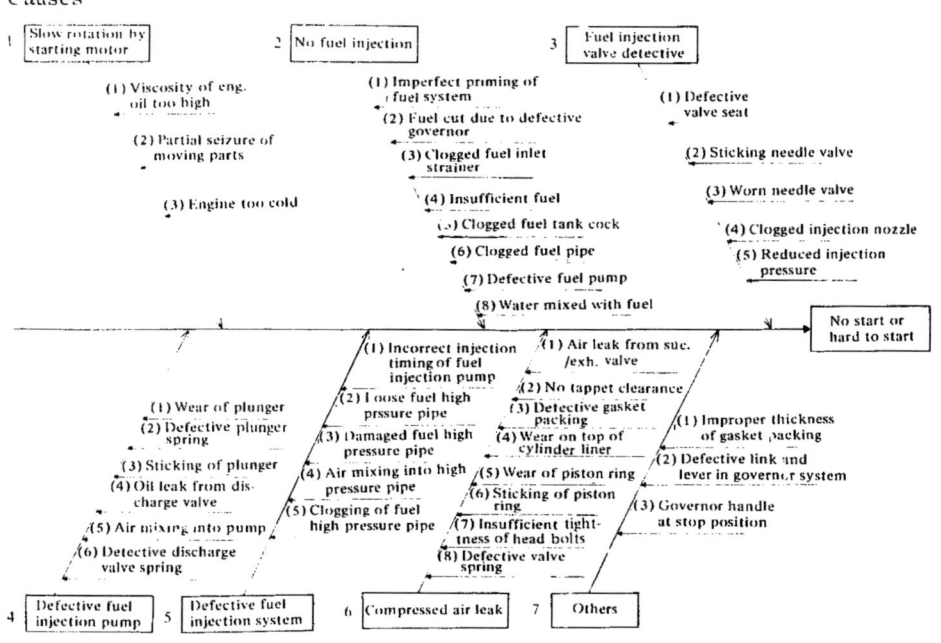

- 46 -

## Measures

| Causes | Measures | Causes | Measures |
|---|---|---|---|
| 1–1 | Warm engine oil or change | 4–4 | Reinstall valve |
| 1–2 | Disassemble and adjust | 4–5 | Vent air |
| 1–3 | Warm up | 4–6 | Change |
| 2–1 | Prime system | 5–1 | Readjust |
| 2–2 | Readjust | 5–2 | Tighten firmly |
| 2–3 | Remove dirt/grease | 5–3 | Change |
| 2–4 | Fill fuel tank | 5–4 | Vent air |
| 2–5 | Open cock | 5–5 | Clean or replace with new one. |
| 2–6 | Clean | | |
| 2–7 | Disassemble and adjust or change part | 6–1 | Re-seat valve |
| | | 6–2 | Readjust |
| 2–8 | Remove water by draining fuel pipe and prime system | 6–3 | Change |
| | | 6–4 | Change |
| | | 6–5 | Change |
| 3–1 | Change part | 6–6 | Disassemble and adjust, or change. |
| 3–2 | Change part | 6–7 | Tighten head bolts evenly |
| 3–3 | Change | 6–8 | Change |
| 3–4 | Clean injection hole or change | | |
| 3–5 | Readjust | 7–1 | Change |
| | | 7–2 | Readjust |
| 4–1 | Change setting of plunger and barrel | 7–3 | Shift the governor handle to higher speed position |
| 4–2 | Change | | |
| 4–3 | Disassemble and adjust, or change | | |

## (2) When power is insufficient:

### Causes

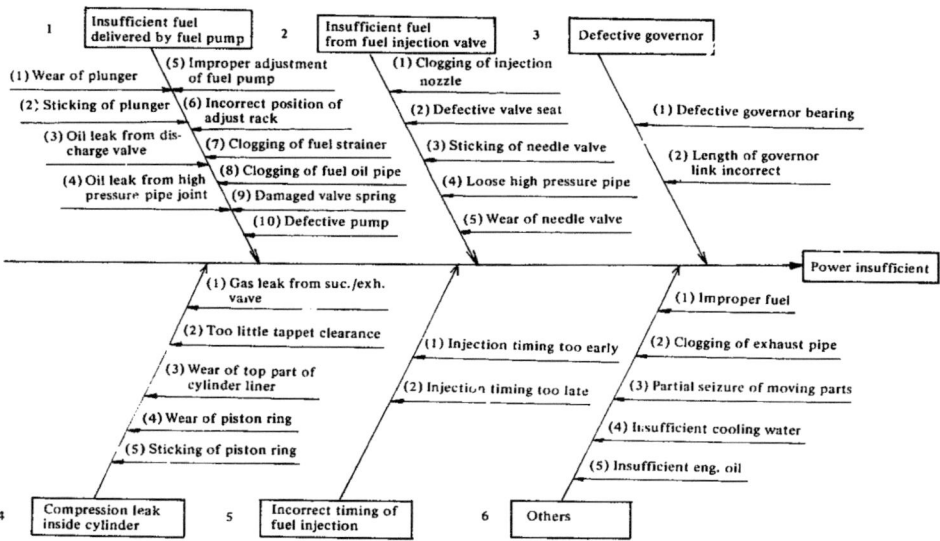

### Measures

| Causes | Measures | Causes | Measures |
|---|---|---|---|
| 1–1 | Change | 4–1 | Re-seat valve |
| 1–2 | Disassemble and adjust, or change | 4–2 | Readjust |
|  |  | 4–3 | Change |
| 1–3 | Reinstall valve | 4–4 | Change |
| 1–4 | Tighten firmly | 4–5 | Disassemble and adjust, or change |
| 1–5 | Readjust |  |  |
| 1–6 | Readjust |  |  |
| 1–7 | Clean | 5–1 | Retard injection timing |
| 1–8 | Clean | 5–2 | Advance timing |
| 1–9 | Change |  |  |
| 1–10 | Repair | 6–1 | Replace with good oil |
|  |  | 6–2 | Clean |
| 2–1 | Clean injection nozzle or change | 6–3 | Disassemble and adjust |
|  |  | 6–4 | Re-seat the suction and discharge valves of cooling water pump |
| 2–2 | Reinstall or change |  |  |
| 2–3 | Reinstall or change |  |  |
| 2–4 | Tighten firmly | 6–5 | Disassemble and clean lubricating oil pump and strainer |
| 2–5 | Change |  |  |
| 3–1 | Change |  |  |
| 3–2 | Repair |  |  |

(3) When engine r.p.m. is not smooth:

Causes

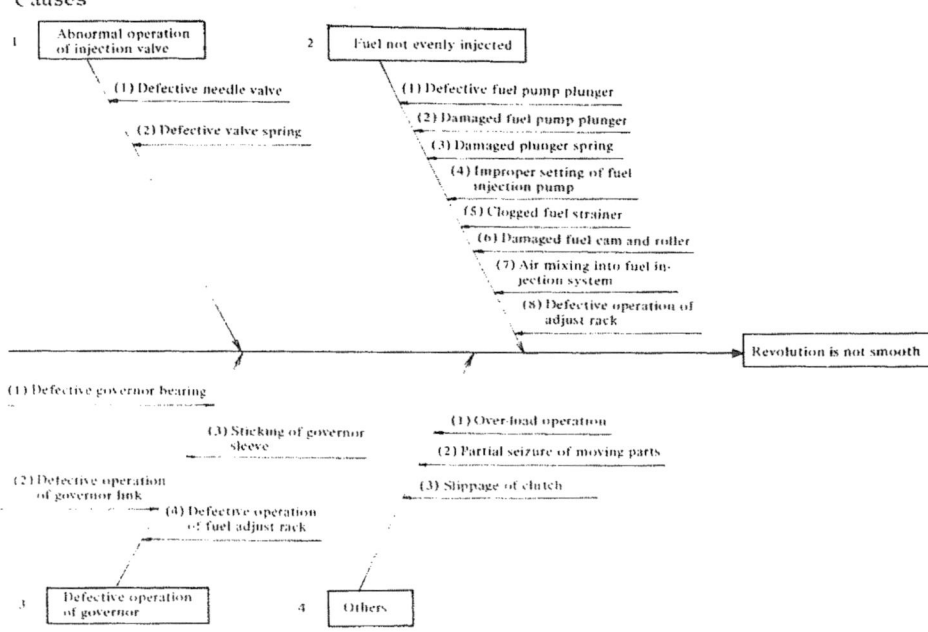

Measures

| Causes | Measures | Causes | Measures |
|---|---|---|---|
| 1-1 | Change part | 2-8 | Repair |
| 1-2 | Change | | |
| | | 3-1 | Change |
| 2-1 | Clean | 3-2 | Repair |
| 2-2 | Change | 3-3 | Clean and adjust |
| 2-3 | Change | 3-4 | Disassemble, clean, and adjust |
| 2-4 | Set pump correctly | | |
| 2-5 | Clean | 4-1 | Reduce load |
| 2-6 | Change | 4-2 | Disassemble and adjust |
| 2-7 | Vent air and prime system | 4-3 | Check and repair |

## (4) When engine knock occurs:

### Causes

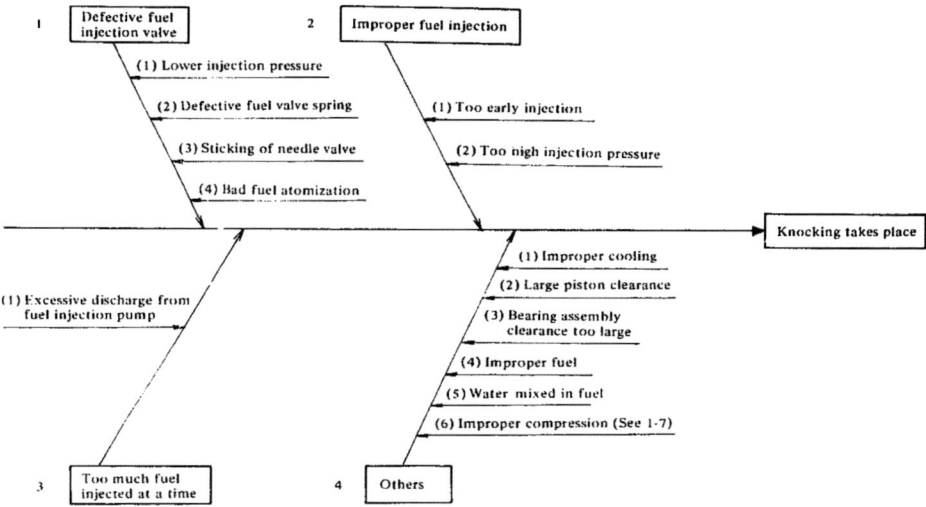

### Measures

| Causes | Measures | Causes | Measures |
|---|---|---|---|
| 1-1 | Adjust for higher injection pressure | 3-1 | Readjust the pump adjust rack |
| 1-2 | Change | 4-1 | Check cooling water pump and valve |
| 1-3 | Disassemble and fit | | |
| 1-4 | Disassemble and clean, or replace | 4-2 | Change |
| | | 4-3 | Change |
| 2-1 | Retard injection timing | 4-4 | Replace with proper fuel |
| 2-2 | Adjust to specified injection pressure | 4-5 | Replace with proper fuel |
| | | 4-6 | Check and adjust |

## (5) When engine stops suddenly

### Causes

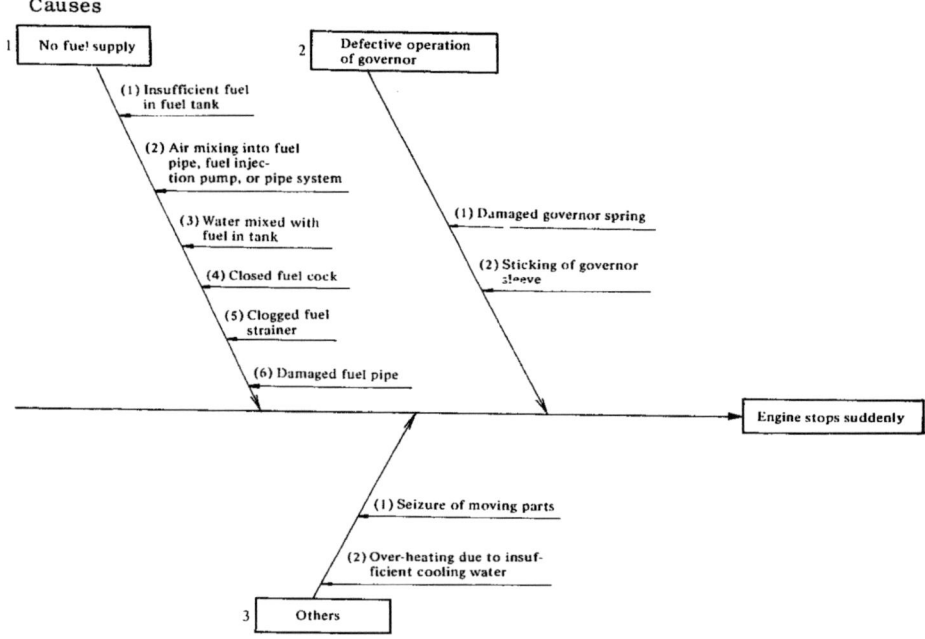

### Measures

| Causes | Measures | Causes | Measures |
|---|---|---|---|
| 1−1 | Refill fuel tank and prime system | 2−1 | Change |
| 1−2 | Vent air | 2−2 | Clean and adjust |
| 1−3 | Drain fuel tank and pipe through drain hole and prime system. | 3−1 | Adjust or change |
| 1−4 | Check and repair, if necessary | 3−2 | Disassemble and adjust cooling water pump and check cooling water pipe |
| 1−5 | Clean | | |
| 1−6 | Change | | |

## (6) Abnormal color of exhaust gas

### Causes

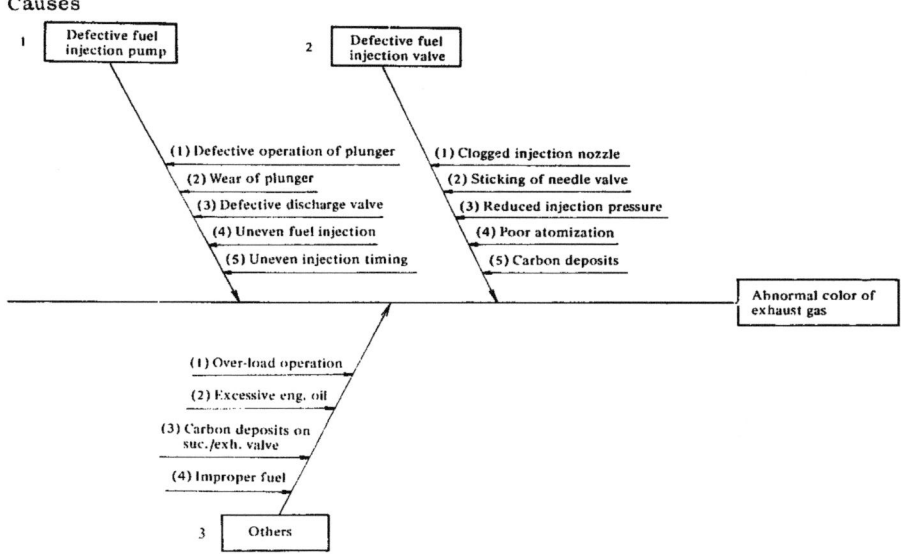

### Measures

| Causes | Measures | Causes | Measures |
|---|---|---|---|
| 1-1 | Check and repair, or change | 2-3 | Readjust |
| 1-2 | Change | 2-4 | Repair or change |
| 1-3 | Check and repair, or change | 2-5 | Clean |
| 1-4 | Readjust | | |
| 1-5 | Readjust | 3-1 | Reduce load |
| | | 3-2 | Adjust oil quantity |
| 2-1 | Clean | 3-3 | Clean |
| 2-2 | Repair or change | 3-4 | Drain and refill fuel tank |

## (7) Other malfunctions
### Causes

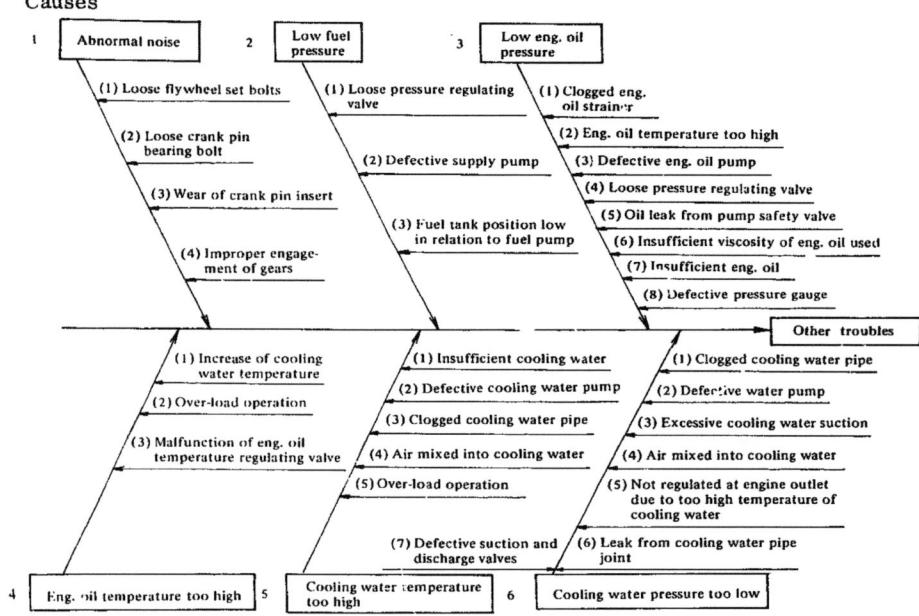

### Measures

| Causes | Measures | Causes | Measures |
|---|---|---|---|
| 1-1 | Tighten nut | 4-1 | Adjust return water flow or check |
| 1-2 | Tighten nut and insert split pin | | And tighten cooling water pump |
| | | 4-2 | Decrease load |
| 1-3 | Remove liner and adjust, or change | 4-3 | Check and adjust |
| 1-4 | Check gears and change, if required. | 5-1 | Increase regulator setting |
| | | 5-2 | Check and repair pump |
| | | 5-3 | Clean |
| 2-1 | Tighten regulating valve | 5-4 | Check suction inlet |
| 2-2 | Check and repair | 5-5 | Decrease load |
| 2-3 | Chagne operating position | | |
| | | 6-1 | Clean |
| 3-1 | Clean | 6-2 | Check and repair pump |
| 3-2 | Increase cooling water flow | 6-3 | Reduce suction or change pump |
| 3-3 | Disassemble and repair, or change | 6-4 | Check suction hole |
| 3-4 | Tighten regulator valve | 6-5 | Rectify cause of increased water temp. and adjust regulator |
| 3-5 | Tighten safety valve | | |
| 3-6 | Change eng. oil | 6-6 | Check and repair |
| 3-7 | Add oil | 6-7 | Check and repair |
| 3-8 | Change | | |

(8) Causes and corrective measures for reduction reversing gear malfunctions

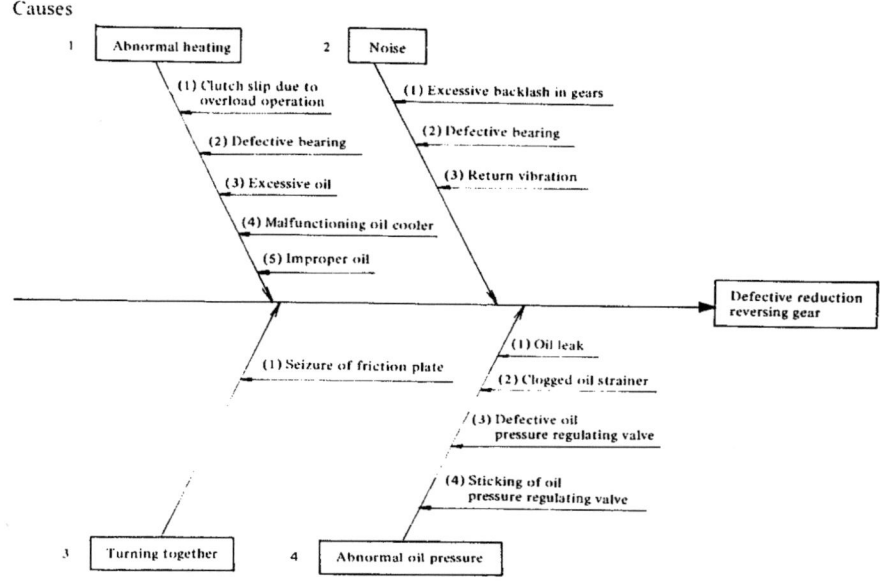

Measures

| Causes | Measures | Causes | Measures |
|---|---|---|---|
| 1-1 | Reduce load | 2-3 | Avoid high r.p.m. with vibration |
| 1-2 | Change | | |
| 1-3 | Check oil quantity and drain to proper level. | 3-1 | Change |
| 1-4 | Adjust minutely | 4-1 | Check and adjust |
| 1-5 | Drain and refill with proper oil | 4-2 | Disassemble and clean |
| | | 4-3 | Change |
| 2-1 | Change | 4-4 | Adjust or change |
| 2-2 | Change | | |

# VII. Fuel Feed Pump (Optional Parts) (720220-52510)

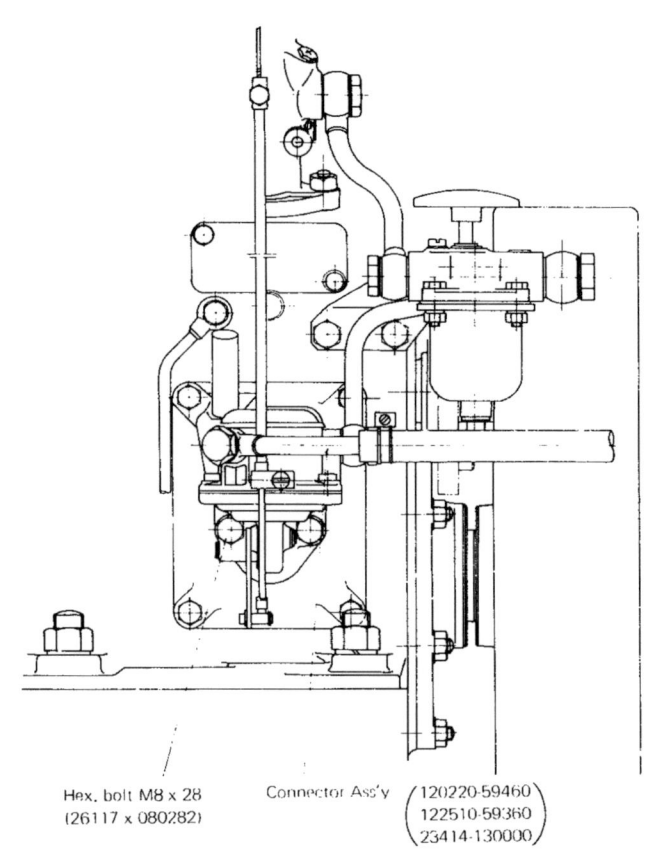

Hex. bolt M8 x 28
(26117 x 080282)

Connector Ass'y (120220-59460)
(122510-59360)
(23414-130000)

A fuel pump is to be installed when location of the fuel tank is not in accordance with the conditions specified by YANMAR. Since the fuel feed pump is an optional item, special ordering is required.

When the Fuel Feed Pump Device is ordered (720220-52510), parts from 1 to 23 shown in the sketch will be delivered.
Refer to the sketch during installation.

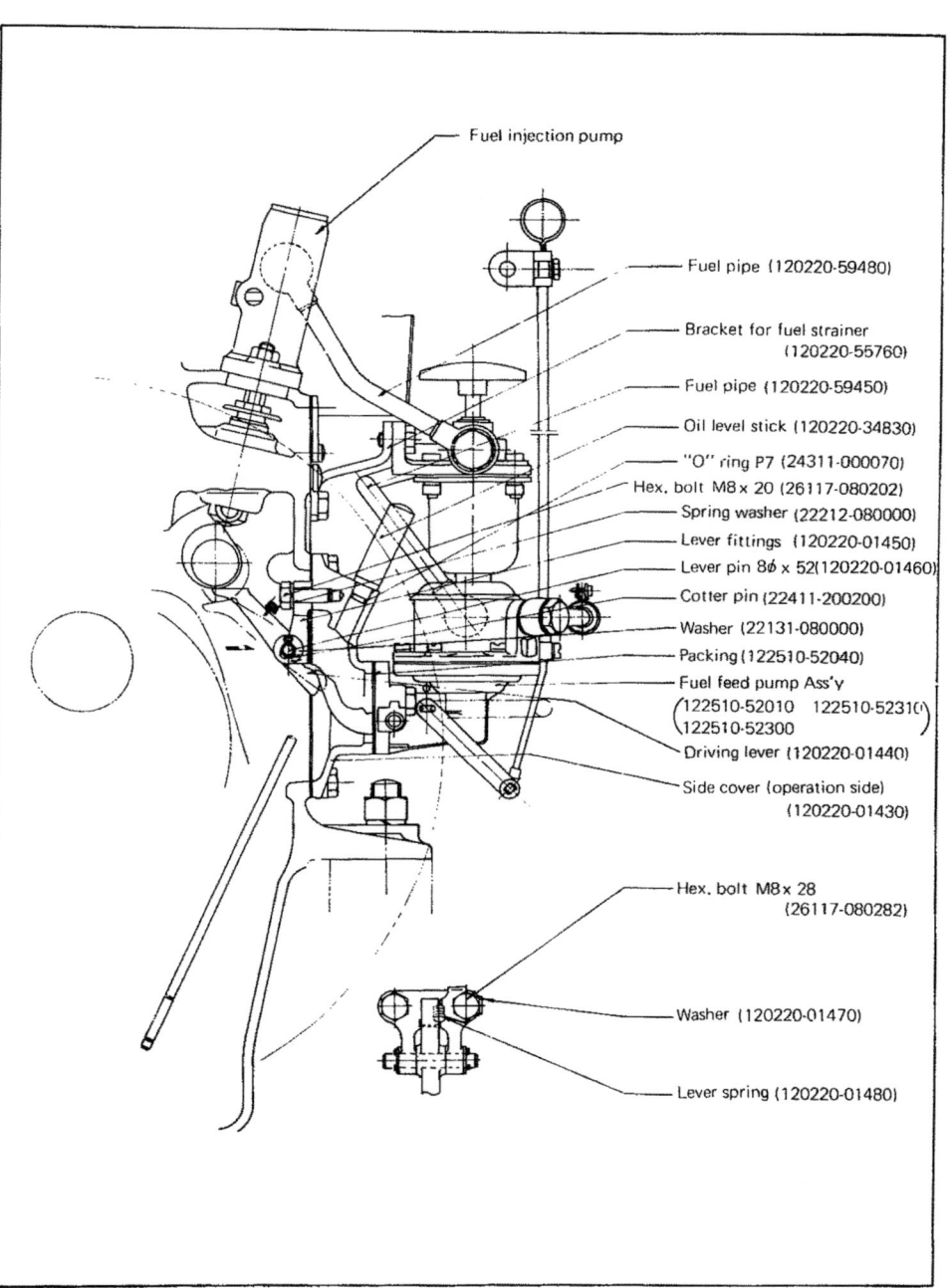

# VIII. List of Approved Oils

(1) APPROVED DIESEL OILS

| Brand | Type |
|---|---|
| SHELL | Shell Diesoline or local equivalent |
| CALTEX | Caltex Diesel Oil |
| MOBIL | Mobil Diesel Oil |
| ESSO | Esso Diesel Oil |
| B·P | B.P. Diesel Oil |

(2) APPROVED LUBRICATING OILS

| Brand | Type | SAE NO. Operating Condition | | | |
|---|---|---|---|---|---|
| | | Below 10°C | 10°～20°C | 20°~35°C | Over 35° |
| SHELL | Shell Rotella Oil | 10W 20/20W | 20/20W | 30 40 | 50 |
| | Shell Talona Oil | 10W | 20 | 30 40 | 50 |
| | Shell Rimula Oil | 20/20W | 20/20W | 30 40 | |
| CALTEX | RPM Delo Marine Oil | 10W | 20 | 30 40 | 50 |
| | RPM Delo Multi-Service-Oil | 20/20W 10W | 20 | 30 40 | 50 |
| | Delvac Special | 10W | 20 | 30 40 | |
| MOBIL | Delvac 20W-40 | 20W-40 | 20W-40 | | |
| | Delvac 1100 Series | 10W 20-20W | 20-20W | 30 40 | 50 |
| | Delvac 1200 Series | 10W 20-20W | 20-20W | 30 40 | 50 |
| ESSO | Estor HD | 10W | 20 | 30 40 | |
| | Esso Lube HD | | 20 | 30 40 | 50 |

| Brand | Type | SAE NO. Operating Condition | | | |
|---|---|---|---|---|---|
| | | Below 10°C | 10°~20°C | 20°~35°C | Over 35° |
| ESSO | Standard Diesel Engine Oil | 10W | 20 | 30<br>40 | 50 |
| B.P. | B.P. Energol ICM<br>B.P. Vanellus<br>B.P. Energol DS3<br>B.P. Vanellus S3 | 20W-30 | 20W-30 | 30<br>40 | 50 |